CW01652175

The Spo

War Cr

Edited by K

Published by Spokesman for the Bertrand Russell Peace Foundation

Spokesman 95 **2007**

CONTENTS

Cover: With thanks to Steve Bell

Printed by the Russell Press Ltd., Nottingham, UK

ISSN 0262 7922 ISBN 0 85124 745 8

Subscriptions
Institutions £35.00
Individuals £20.00 (UK)
£25.00 (ex UK)

Back issues available on request

A CIP catalogue record for this book is available from the British Library

Published by the
Bertrand Russell Peace Foundation Ltd.,
Russell House
Bulwell Lane
Nottingham NG6 0BT
England
Tel. 0115 9784504
email:
elfeuro@compuserve.com
www.spokesmanbooks.com
www.russfound.org

Editorial

War Crimes

On the 3rd April 2007, the Russian News Agency, Novosti, reported a statement by Yuri Baluyevsky, the head of the Russian Armed Forces General Staff. He warned that 'Washington needs to think twice before launching a military campaign against Tehran, as such an attack would have global implications'. The General said that it might be realistic to anticipate that the Americans could inflict damage on Iran's military and industrial potential: 'but winning the war is unachievable – its reverberations would be heard across the world'.

General Baluyevsky said that when deciding upon military action against Iran, the US leadership should bear in mind the negative experience it had garnered in other countries of the region. He warned that if the US goes to war with Iran as well as Afghanistan and Iraq 'the world may see America decline as the world's mightiest and most powerful state'.

Other Russian spokesmen had previously warned of possible American air strikes on April 6th, Good Friday.[1] There have also been repeated warnings by critics of the regime in Washington, not so specific, but pointing up strong possibilities of such military initiatives.[2]

White House spokeswoman, Dana Perino, denied all these stories at a news briefing on Monday 2nd April. The news had been widely reported that the American aircraft carrier, *Nimitz*, with a supporting flotilla of lesser ships, was bound for the Persian Gulf to join other aircraft carrier strike groups already hovering there. The American military claimed that the presence of two major carriers in the Gulf was 'intended to demonstrate US "resolve to build regional security and bring long term stability to the region".'

Previously fifteen British sailors and marines had been detained by Iranian forces, when they were alleged to be operating in Iranian territorial waters.[3] This allegation had been strenuously, even belligerently, denied by Tony Blair, although Craig Murray, the former Ambassador in Tashkent, who was victimised by the Foreign Office for undiplomatically speaking up for human rights in Uzbekistan, offered rather compelling testimony to show that arguments about the positioning of the frontier between Iraqi and Iranian territorial waters were somewhat metaphysical in nature.

Before his time in Tashkent, Mr. Murray spent several years in a basement in Whitehall, seeking to determine maritime boundaries for the Foreign and Commonwealth Office. He had been personally responsible in the Embargo Surveillance Centre for getting 'individual real time clearance for the Royal Navy to board specific vessels in these waters'. He says of the present dispute:

> 'As I feared, Blair adopted the stupid and confrontational approach of publishing maps ignoring the boundaries dispute, thus claiming a very blurred situation is crystal clear and the Iranians totally in the wrong.'

Mr. Murray continues:

> 'Tony Blair's contempt for Middle Eastern lives has already been adequately demonstrated in Iraq and Lebanon. His lack of genuine concern for British servicemen is demonstrated by his steadfast refusal to meet even one parent of a dead British serviceman or woman killed in the wars he created.'

Apparently the boundary line between the waters of Iraq and Iran is based upon an extrapolation of the boundary which divides the Shatt Al-Arab Waterway. This boundary shifts with the shifting banks of the Waterway itself, so that manifestly its extension can be subject to important variations. As Murray tells us, the *Stars and Stripes* magazine (October 24th 2006) reports:

> 'Bumping into the Iranians cannot be helped in the Northern Persian Gulf, where the lines between Iraqi and Iranian territorial water are blurred … No maritime border has been agreed upon by the two countries, explained Royal Australian Navy Commodore Peter Lockwood, the Commander of the Combined Task Force in the Northern Persian Gulf.'

None of these considerations inhibited the rhetoric of Mr. Blair. President Bush, however, was even less restrained. He called the detainees 'hostages', a term which not even the British had evoked.

At the time of writing, although we are very agnostic about the anticipated Good Friday aerial bombardment of Iran, and although we remain hopeful of a diplomatic solution to the argument about the detention of British military personnel, it is clear that events are very mobile, and that rationality dawns very much in fits and starts among some of the senior personnel. Is there any evidence that the British diplomats and top military brass have been able to restrain Mr. Blair, or lock him in a cellar until the dispute is satisfactorily settled? Fortunately, he will soon be gone, but these contemporary crises do show that we remain in rather dire danger right up to the actual point of his departure.

For a long time we have tended towards the opinion that the extension of American hostilities into Iran was improbable for the very reason given by Yuri Baluyevsky. Even if the realities of the power balance may elude President Bush, it is perfectly evident that large numbers of senior American statesmen, not to say Generals and diplomats, have a greatly more realistic appreciation of the balance of military force. Long ago, we reported the judicious assessment of General Odom, of the effects of the American conquest of Iraq, which, he said, had strengthened America's enemies, revived Al Qaeda, and made Iran the unchallenged power in the region.

Even if the weight of informed opinion in Washington may not be quite enough to cancel the aggravated imbecility of the man in the White House, there is the further weight of America's allies. Saudi Arabia, in particular, is expressing open criticism of war talk against Iran. If the neo-cons were to succeed in unleashing the malnourished dogs of their wars on Tehran, they could wind up not only strengthening the Iranians, but fatally undermining their long-term Middle Eastern allies.

There was once a time when a famous strategist declared that 'imperialism and all reactionaries are paper tigers'. We took leave to doubt this presumption when it was fashionable in some places. But due to the exertions of Mr Bush, ably assisted by Mr. Blair, it almost begins to be true.

We are about to see the end of the Blair administration. The elections at the beginning of May 2007 give rise to dismal forecasts about the prospects for the Labour Party, and it is generally presumed that the Prime Minister will make his farewells shortly after those elections, while there may remain two or three supporters to whom he can bid goodbye. Our grief will not be measureless, and many people may even share in the sense of relief which will accompany Mr. Blair's departure.

But a judicious assessment of the events which have given rise to this dismal balance sheet will most probably reflect the wisdom of the title chosen by Judge Thomas of the Supreme Court of New Zealand, for his magisterial paper. We have been persuaded to publish this text, because it is not only 'an indictment of Tony Blair', but also because it documents 'the failure of the political process' which has given rise to the horrors in Iraq, and a major crisis of confidence in Government and democratic institutions more widely. Where does the writ of the democratic process run, when that process has been so widely travestied, ignored, and even violated?

The cogent case for impeachment of the Prime Minister was made in England by a group of British Parliamentarians, led by the spokesmen of the Welsh and Scottish Nationalist Parties. A debate was secured by Plaid Cymru and the Scottish National Party, and supported by a cross-Party coalition of members. One hundred and sixty-four signatures were obtained for Early Day Motion 1088, *Conduct of Government Policy in Relation to the War against Iraq*. Among these were thirty-three Labour members, sixty Conservatives and fifty-nine Liberal Democrats. Adam Price MP explained the thinking behind this motion:

> 'Three and a half years on and Iraq is mired in blood, and the shocking figures published recently show that the death toll has reached 655,000. Neither the Hutton nor Butler Inquiries addressed the question if the Parliament and country were misled into this bloody conflict. I believe that it is essential for the credibility of our democracy that we establish what combination of deception, delusion and ineptitude carried us down this fateful path.
>
> This debate is not about revisiting old ground, it is an urgent attempt to restore the balance of power between Parliament and the Executive; and of the utmost contemporary relevance if we are to prevent such tragedies from happening again. It will probably be the first and last occasion to restore proper accountability of Government.'

He was supported by Alex Salmond, SNP Leader:

> 'This debate offers MPs a second chance – a chance to re-establish Parliamentary accountability over an executive who has led the country into a bloody quagmire – and a last chance to change strategy and direction on the disastrous course of events in Iraq.
>
> If this motion carries – or indeed even if it records a substantial shift in opinion since the vote which took us to war – Mr. Blair's time in Downing Street will be numbered in days, not weeks or months.'

The text of the motion is based on Early Day Motion 1088:

> 'That this House believes that there should be a select committee of seven honourable Members, being members of Her Majesty's Privy Council, to review the way in which the responsibilities of government were discharged in relation to Iraq and all matters relevant thereto, in the period leading up to military action in that country in March 2003 and in its aftermath.'

But here we now have the considered opinion of a senior Judge from New Zealand, who, weighing every word, offers us conclusions and refreshing candour long missing in British official pronouncements.

'I believe that the forty-five minute claim had to be a knowing lie'. How many British Ministers and senior public servants must have known this? How many Judges must have swallowed deeply, and found more decorous descriptions to cover it? And how many British people have pondered the implications in deep frustration? Deliberate lies at the head of Government annul the foundations of trust by the governed, and lower all official thinking to new levels of duplicity and hypocrisy.

Judge Thomas has laid down a powerful challenge. 'The shortcomings in the political process are self-evident', he says, 'in that the Prime Minister was not constrained from committing the above political, immoral and illegal misdemeanours, nor has he been held accountable for them.'

Until accountability is reimposed, we cannot re-establish honest, political discourse. Evidently politicians have told lies before. But now we live with untruths that cannot be corrected, with falsehoods that have become official. Where the lie rules, logic itself gives way to unreason.

Ken Coates

Footnotes

1 Colonel General Leonid Ivashov, Vice President of the Academy of Geo-political Sciences, warned that 'The Pentagon is planning to deliver a massive air strike on Iran's military infrastructure in the near future'. Andre Uglanov reported in *Arguments and Facts* that he expected an onslaught from various bases, including Diego Garcia and the aircraft carriers currently deployed in the Persian Gulf. He cited Ivashov as anticipating an American attack, 'or more precisely a violent action against Iran'.

2 See, notably, the recent statements by Seymour Hersh and Scott Ritter.

3 Since these words were written, a dramatic announcement was made by President Ahmadinejad at the end of a discourse on recent foreign policy developments. He ceremonially decorated the Revolutionary Guards who had captured the fifteen British sailors and marines, and then announced their imminent and unconditional release. They had been pardoned he said, in commemoration of the birthday of the prophet Muhammad, of Easter, and of the Passover. Kitted out with new suits presented by the Iranian authorities, the fifteen, laden with presents, were flown out of Tehran the next morning. Mr. Blair celebrated the return of the British captives with a number of ungracious remarks, implying but not alleging that other servicemen and women who had been killed that day owed their deaths to Iranian weaponry. The evidence for this proposition has not yet been produced, and it may well be found alongside the weapons of mass destruction which took Britain to war against Iraq four bloodthirsty years ago.

Kurt Vonnegut

Just as we were going to print, we learned with very great sadness of the death of Kurt Vonnegut who, in addition to all his other merits, was a great and consistent support for *The Spokesman*. We shall all miss him deeply, for his encouragement, his jokes, his innumerable faxes, and his unfailing help. He waged a one-man campaign to promote Trevor Griffiths's screenplay on Tom Paine, *These Are the Times*, which we published in 2005, and his wide circle of friends were bombarded with entreaties to help get this film made. We shall celebrate his life in our next number, and invite his friends to write in. We send our condolences to Jill Krementz and their family.

One of Kurt Vonnegut's faxes

Indicting Tony Blair

A Judgment by Judge Thomas
of the Supreme Court of New Zealand

Introduced by Alice Mahon

With comments by
Alex Salmond MP, Adam Price MP
and Richard Horton of *The Lancet*

Introduction

'I bitterly regret not supporting the impeachment of Tony Blair'

Alice Mahon

We should be grateful to Judge Thomas for his brilliant analysis, 'An Indictment of Tony Blair, the Prime Minister of Great Britain, and the Failure of the Political Process.'

As a Labour MP, I along with other colleagues opposed the war. I organised inside and outside parliament, forming and chairing the Iraq Liaison Committee, which brought together MPs across the political spectrum. I met Tony Blair and other members of the Cabinet on a number of occasions in a vain attempt to persuade them that any military intervention based upon such flimsy evidence would lead to massive loss of life and appalling consequences for the people of the region. At every level we were told Saddam was a threat to the world and that he had weapons of mass destruction.

In many heated exchanges with the Prime Minister I have to say he never once accepted an argument against the military option.

In spring 2002 I sponsored the first early day motion against the war. I had spoken to journalists who had accompanied Tony Blair on the now infamous visit to the Bush ranch in Texas. They were convinced that Blair had pledged his support for war on that visit. I believed them even though Downing Street denied that any decision had been taken, and it is my belief that they continuously and deliberately lied to MPs, the media, and the country. The decision to go to war had been taken.

It is good to see the whole presentation and the content of the 'dodgy dossier' dissected legally, and elegantly rubbished. It is also good to see the Prime Minister's theatrical assertions about the reality of weapons of mass destruction exposed for the shallow spin that it really was.

I spoke at the biggest protest rally ever seen in this country, and right up to the vote on going to war, I used what little influence I had to try to prevent it. All to no avail. Blair was determined to go to war. He was not concerned about the illegality, after all he had got away with it in Yugoslavia, which was also an illegal war, and

Alice Mahon visited New Zealand and brought us the extraordinary analysis by Judge Thomas (see below). She was MP for Halifax from 1987 to 2005.

in his own words he was willing to 'pay the blood price'.

What a bloody price that has been. A country destroyed, 600,000 of its people killed, millions more who have fled the violence or have been ethnically cleansed are refugees in other countries. Nearly 4,000 allied troops are dead and thousands have been sent home with hideous injuries, and yet Tony Blair is still Prime Minister and it is said that as soon as he retires he will earn millions as he tours the rich man's world boasting about his exploits.

How can this be right?

War crimes on a massive scale have been committed in his name since the invasion. Remember Fallujah. The first assault on Fallujah was reported by Al Jazeera. The world saw the brutality of the US forces and Bush had to withdraw his troops.

The second assault, which took place in November 2004, did not have Al Jazerra to act as a witness as they had been banned from reporting in Iraq by the puppet government of Allawi.

The United States claimed that the city was an insurgent enclave and they ordered the city to be evacuated. However, it is widely agreed that between 30,000 and 50,000 civilians were left in the city, but that did not stop the military treating Fallujah as if its only inhabitants were insurgents. The US military destroyed thousands of homes, illegally denied civilians access to the Red Cross and, according to the United Nations' special rapporteur, 'used hunger and deprivation as a weapon of war against the civilian population'. Under the Geneva Conventions these actions are war crimes. These, however, were not the only war crimes committed in Fallujah.

In Fallujah the United States military used white phosphorus, a chemical weapon. According to reporter Darrin Mortensen working for a San Diego newspaper who was embedded with the US military,

> 'Cpl. Nicholas Bogart, a US marine, directed his men to fire round after round of high explosives and white phosphorus into the city for two days, never knowing what the targets were or what damage the resulting explosions caused'.

There is other evidence of the use of white phosphorus. In his documentary 'Fallujah – The Hidden Massacre', Sigfredo Ranucci, an Italian producer working for RAI, a public broadcasting company, documented in graphic detail the horror that was Fallujah.

I asked the Ministry of Defence twice if chemical weapons had been used in Fallujah, and twice the Ministry of Defence denied they had been used. In June 2005, two months after I had left Parliament, my successor Linda Riordan received a letter from Adam Ingram admitting that they had been used.

Who will be held responsible for these war crimes? And how do we answer Judge Thomas's claim? He says:

> 'both Parliament and the Labour Party have failed the democratic imperative. Tony Blair, in foreign policy, exerted unbridled and unchecked power to pursue his personal vision. When that vision was threatened he was able to manipulate the political process to his own ends.'

He is absolutely correct, the Executive through the power of the whips control Parliament. The Prime Minister and a handful of close advisers control Party Conference.

At the 2002 conference great efforts were made by myself and others to be called to speak. The New Labour organisers went to extraordinary lengths to stop any one with an anti-war position from speaking. It was only after I had made a real nuisance of myself and the trade union sector kept shouting my name that I was eventually called.

That was the last real debate about Iraq at Conference for delegates. The foreign affairs and defence debates are now so tightly controlled that, in 2005, my friend Walter Wolfgang was thrown out and arrested for shouting 'rubbish' at Jack Straw.

With many others I believe that Tony Blair and George Bush should be held to account for visiting this appalling horror on the Iraqi people. I bitterly regret not supporting the impeachment of Tony Blair, but I concur with and support this excellent analysis put forward by Judge Thomas.

An indictment of Tony Blair, and the failure of the political process

Judge E W Thomas

E W Thomas is a Retired Judge of the Court of Appeal of New Zealand; Acting Judge of the Supreme Court of New Zealand; and Distinguished Visiting Fellow at the Law School at the University of Auckland. He is author of The Judicial Process: Realism, Pragmatism, Practical Reasoning and Principles *(Cambridge University Press 2005).*

Terrorism has undoubtedly put a strain upon democratic institutions, the democratic process and basic democratic precepts. Many people are concerned that the effectiveness of the political process has been eroded and that the rule of law and fundamental human rights and civil liberties have been placed in jeopardy. They are troubled by the feeling that democracy is more fragile and their freedoms more precarious than previously thought.

Some look to the judiciary to maintain the rule of law and protect human rights and civil liberties. But it is axiomatic that the rule of law and human rights and, indeed, democracy itself, will not survive, much less flourish, if the only safeguard is to be found in the legal system. The judiciary's power and influence is limited, especially in a legal system where the judges are regularly reminded by lawyers, legal academics, political scientists, politicians, writers of letters to the editor and others to accept obeisance to the Diceyean concept of parliamentary sovereignty. Primary responsibility for the preservation of the rule of law and human rights, and accountability for any departure from the rule of law or breach of those rights, must exist within the political system. Unless that political responsibility is discharged democracy, or the kind of democracy the people esteem, is in danger of being undermined.

I am not satisfied that, in this age of terrorism, the probity of government and the ability of democratic institutions is adequate to prevent serious inroads into the rule of law, or to monitor the boundary between human rights and their breach or, indeed, to safeguard and secure the democratic process. Nor am I satisfied that those politicians who seek to redefine the rule of law, or who cross the boundary between the observance of human rights and their breach, or who show less than constitutional respect for the democratic process will be effectively held to account for their default.

For the purpose of testing this hypothesis I

propose to examine Tony Blair's role leading up to the war in Iraq. Focusing on Tony Blair does not mean that I am unaware of, or indifferent to, the greater involvement of the President of the United States and his administration. George W Bush's conduct has been canvassed in any number of articles and books.[1] He does not emerge unscathed. But the fact that the policies and behaviour of the Bush administration are in many respects more extreme than the policies and behaviour of Mr Blair cannot excuse the latter from scrutiny. He may properly be judged in his own right.

Rather than essay a broad sweep of events leading up to the war I have selected a number of key matters to explore, and to finally demonstrate, Mr Blair's level of culpability. These matters comprise the sudden shift in the claim that Iraq had the potential to develop weapons of mass destruction to the claim that Iraq actually possessed weapons of mass destruction; the manipulation of the intelligence provided by the intelligence services in preparing the first dossier; the misrepresentation that Iraq had the capacity to deliver missiles carrying weapons of mass destruction within 45 minutes; the misuse of the Attorney-General's advice relating to the legality of the war; the forgiving tolerance of the use of torture on terrorist suspects; and the condoning of a doomed post-war economic strategy. I seek to bring a judicial approach to this examination. An analysis of the extent to which human rights have been imperilled by the Prime Minister's behaviour is then briefly undertaken. I conclude by emphasizing the failure of the political process to effectively monitor the Prime Minister's foreign policy and to properly hold him to account.

In approaching this examination, my pre-disposition was to believe that Mr Blair was deluded, but sincere in his belief. After considerable reading and much reflection, however, my final conclusion is that Mr Blair deliberately and repeatedly misled Cabinet, Parliament, the British Labour Party and the people in a number of respects. It is not possible to hold that he was simply deluded but sincere; a victim of his own self-deception. His deception was deliberate.

I admit to having personally found the extent of the manipulation and distortion of the democratic system and lack of accountability profoundly disturbing. Exercising a presidential style of rule, obtaining no effective policy input from Cabinet or Parliament and shrouding the development of Iraq policy in secrecy, Mr Blair was effectively free to determine Britain's foreign policy as if it were his personal fiefdom.

1 See, e.g. Graydon Carter, *What We've Lost: How the Bush Administration has Curtailed Freedoms, Ravaged the Environment and Damaged America and the World* (Little, Brown, 2004); Seymour M. Hersh, *Chain of Command: The Road form 9/11 to Abu Ghraib* (Allen Lane an imprint of Penguin Books, 2004); Jack Huberman, *The Bush-Hater's Handbook: An A-Z Guide to the Most Appalling Presidency of the Past 100 Years* (Granta books, London, 2004); Molly Ivins, *Who Let the Dogs In? A Personal History of America's Most Incredible Political Animals* (Allison & Busby Limited, 2004); Richard A. Clarke, *Against all Enemies: Inside America's War on Terror* (Free Press, 2004); Bob Woodward, *State of Denial: Bush at War, Part III* (Simon & Schuster, 2006); Sidney Blumenthal, *How Bush Rules: Chronicles of a Radical Regime* (Princeton University Press, 2006): Thomas E. Ricks, *Fiasco: The American Military Adventure in Iraq* (Allen Lane, an imprint of Penguin Books, 2006).

Support for neo-conservative policies

For reasons which remain obscure or contentious, Mr Blair chose to endorse the neo-conservative, ideologically based policies of the Bush administration. His truckling support for the policies of that administration cannot be entirely explained by his predisposition to bring about a new 'global order'.[2]

Take, for example, the Prime Minister's assertion when seeking to brand anti-war sentiment prior to the invasion as 'anti-Americanism' that he firmly believed 'America is a force for good'.[3] Examined even cursorily, the assertion is specious. The issue is not whether America is a force for good but whether America, led by a neo-conservative and ideological administration bent on a war against Iraq, is a force for good. Far right thinking which would be unacceptable in the domestic sphere does not mystically gain in rationality when transferred to the international arena. Thinking which is divorced from reality and crude in its simplicity does not become more realistic, less ideological and better informed simply because it emanates from the President of the United States and the administration he has chosen.

David Cameron, the leader of the Opposition, no doubt sensitive to the direction of public opinion, has recently observed that much of the Bush administration's thinking was 'unrealistic and simplistic'.[4] Why, then, was Tony Blair not able to perceive this unrealistic and simplistic thinking before committing the United Kingdom to a tragic and disastrous war? Literally millions of people around the globe shared this perception long before the invasion. The might of the United States, it was commonly said, would win the immediate war but it would not win the peace. In the result, Mr Blair's close alliance with the Bush administration vested its policies with a veneer of 'respectability'. The neo-conservative and ideological underpinnings of the decision to invade Iraq were obscured. Indeed, the phrase 'coalition of the willing' would have sounded silly without the involvement of Great Britain.

Christopher Meyer, the British Ambassador in the United States leading up to the war, in his book, *DC Confidential: The Controversial Memoirs of a British Ambassador at the Time of 9/11 and the Iraq War,*[5] paints a picture of Mr Blair as being over-awed by the President and his administration.[6] He observes that Tony Blair always appeared seduced by the proximity and glamour of American power. He perceptively points out that, in adopting the moral high ground and the pure white flame of unconditional support of an ally, the Prime Minister placed himself in the hands of that ally. Mr Blair was fêted by the Bush administration from the

2 Steven Kettell, *Dirty Politics? New Labour, British Democracy and the Invasion of Iraq* (Zed Books, London & New York, 2006), at pp 5, 43-35 and 182.

3 Repeated as a mantra; see, e.g. *BBC News*, Mark Mardell, BBC Chief Correspondent, 2 April, 2003.

4 When distinguishing his perception of conservatism from neo-conservatism, i.e. the Bush administration's world view, Mr Cameron said that they [the 'sound-bites' that led up to the war in Iraq] were 'unrealistic and simplistic'. See David Cameron's 9/11 speech; *BBC News*, 11/9/06 (news.bbc.co.uk/1 /hi/uk_politics/5333406.stm).

5 Weidenfield & Nicolson, London, 2005.

6 Bruce Anderson, 'Why US has lost the plot in Iraq', New Zealand Herald, 30 October, 2006. See also Blumenthal, *How Bush Rules*, supra n 1, p 284.

outset. He was accorded personal attention, praise, privileges and honours few, if any, British Prime Ministers have received in the United States. His speeches dedicating Great Britain to unconditional solidarity with the United States made him an 'American hero'.[7] Certainly, Mr Blair's deference was exceptional.[8] After a time one nurtures the feeling that this over-awed deference may have had a psychological element blinding him to the reality. Whether a causative link can be established between the coddling and adulation which he received and his exceptional deference is problematic, but there can be no doubt that Mr Blair consistently failed to display the independence one would expect of the leader of a sovereign nation.[9]

Mr Blair's appreciation of neo-conservatism is also seemingly vagarious. In response to criticism directed at his indiscriminate support for the Bush administration he is reported to have said: 'It is apparently a "neo-conservative", i.e. right wing view, to be ardently in favour of spreading democracy round the world'.[10] Again, this statement is superficial. Even as a debating point it is self-evidently weak. Most people, many ardently so, are in favour of spreading democracy around the world, more particularly if it is indigenous to the culture of the country concerned. That goal is not in dispute, although the view that democracy can be exported on American and British mortars may have died a thousand deaths in Iraq. What critics' dispute is that the war should have been embarked upon by what was, effectively, a Prime Ministerial fiat based on unverified, false or fabricated evidence. What they urge is that it was impulsively foolhardy to support a war inspired by the Bush administration's suspect motives; criminal folly to make war without being assured that the peace could be won; devious to lend support to the pretence that the war was a war on terrorism or terror and not a straight out war against Iraq; naïve to minimize the problem of imposing a western style sectarian democracy from without; and disingenuous to undertake the invasion underestimating the difficulties the coalition would face, the level of resistance that would be encountered, the casualties and cost in human terms, the potential for war to brutalise its participants, and the damage to the relationship of Islam and the western world.

---

7 Blumenthal, *How Bush Rules*, supra n 1, p 205.

8 Ibid, at pp 34-36 and 189-191.

9 E.g. Mr Blair generally went along with Mr Bush's shifting justifications for the war: from its possession of actual WMD to its possession of WMD programmes to its WMD-related programmes and, finally, to its WMD-related programme activities. Further, see Riddell, *Hug Them Close: Blair, Clinton, Bush, and the 'Special Relationship'* (Politicos; London, 2004) pp 280-281; and Bob Woodward, *Plan of Attack* (Simon & Schuster, 2004) pp 434-435. Similarly, when two trucks containing sophisticated equipment were located on Iraq in June 2003, Bush was quick to claim that weapons of mass destruction had been discovered. The rest of the world was yawningly sceptical and waited for the full facts to emerge. But Tony Blair immediately claimed the 'our experts' had found 'two K 119 Facilities'. Of course, as widely anticipated, the claim was false. When examined three days later it was ascertained that the trucks contained equipment for the production of helium for weather balloons. Yet again, the Prime Minister had seemingly accepted the Washington line as if it were gospel. The examples of blind support are endless.

10 Tony Blair, speech to the Foreign Policy Centre quoted in full in *The Guardian*, 21 March, 2006. See also http://politics.guardian.co.uk/iraq/story/0,,1736105,00.html#article_continue

Nowhere is the folly of following the neo-conservative, ideologically driven Bush administration's policies more apparent than in the Prime Minister's endorsement of that administration's war model. The war model was not only unwise, it was misconceived.[11] It is a false and dangerous metaphor; false because it assumes that there can be a war against an abstraction, such as terror, and dangerous because it is prone to be taken literally. Thus, the catchphrase fostered the notion that the so-called war on terror required a military response relying on military might.[12] The problem of terrorism was conflated with that of 'rogue states' and weapons of mass destruction, and this conflation was blatantly used to sanction the invasion of Iraq.[13] Seemingly absent was any appreciation that a military response would fuel future violence, create conditions of social and political injustice, out of which extreme movements would emerge, and quickly antagonize the more moderate voices that might otherwise prevail.[14] Similarly absent, almost criminally so, was any realistic understanding of the religious, ethnic, nationalistic and tribal forces at work in Iraq which would render the war a disastrous military operation.[15]

Long before September 11 Tony Blair had an ambition to reassert Britain's position as a 'global player' on the international stage and it seems that, as part of this global vision, he was in favour of regime change in Iraq prior to the advent of the Bush administration.[16] Mr Blair was therefore receptive to the ill-conceived war model, and there can be little doubt that in late 2001 or early 2002 he gave George W Bush a firm assurance that the invasion would have Britain's solid backing.[17] Following a meeting in February 2002, the United States and British attacks on the Iraqi no-fly zone were intensified. At a press conference Mr Bush and Mr Blair presented a united front and reasserted their joint commitment to resolve the threat Iraq was perceived to pose.[18] Then, in April, the Prime Minister

11 For a compelling condemnation of the notion of the so-called war on terror, see George Soros, *The Age of Fallibility: The Consequences of the War on Terror* (Weidenfeld & Nicolson, London, 2006), pp 101-111.

12 The phrase 'war on terror' was first used by Mr Bush on 20 September 2001. http:www.whitehouse.gov/news/releases/2001/09/20010920-8.html.

13 As, of course, it was also used to sanction Guantanamo Bay. For a compelling condemnation of Guantanamo Bay, see Philippe Sands QC, *Lawless World: The whistle-blowing account of how Bush and Blair are taking the law into their own hands* (Penguin Books, 2006), Chapter 7, 'Guantanamo: the Legal Black Hole', p 143 et seq.

14 It is time to move away from the war model and, indeed, the 'war on terror', the flaws in which are now painfully patent, towards a new model based on respect for the rule of law and human rights, an internationally coordinated anti-terror strategy, independent of American domination or imperialism, and a long term political vision that will reduce the global tensions that generate a political constituency for terrorists. See Richard Ashby Wilson, 'Human Rights in the "War on Terror"' in *Human Rights in the War on Terror*, Ed. Wilson (Cambridge University Press, 2005) 1, at p 33.

15 Thomas Ricks in *Fiasco*, supra n 2, demonstrates that there were many senior officials, high ranking military personnel and public interest organisations that warned the Bush administration of the dangers of a war in Iraq well in advance of the invasion. They were ignored.

16 Kettell, *Dirty Politics*, supra n 2, pp 4-5.

17 It is not possible to fix a firm date. Possibly, the firm backing was given at the White House meeting on 20 September 2001 or at the Camp David Summit in April 2002.

18 Kettell, *Dirty Politics*, supra n 2, p 49.

met Mr Bush at the President's ranch in Texas. The official line, confirmed in a leaked briefing paper, was that the United Kingdom would support military action to bring about regime change subject to the President reinvigorating the Middle East peace process and seeking the endorsement of the United Nations. No doubt recognising the political difficulties faced by the Prime Minister, the President accepted these terms. The die was therefore cast.

There is evidence, however, that Mr Blair's private commitment was even firmer than these developments would indicate. In March 2002, Sir David Manning, the Prime Minister's foreign policy adviser, penned the Prime Minister a memorandum reporting on discussions he had with Condoleezza Rice. Sir David stated he had told Condoleezza Rice that he, Mr Blair, 'would not budge in his support for regime change'. But, it was reaffirmed, the Prime Minister had to 'manage a press, a Parliament and a public opinion that was very different from anything in the States'.[19] John Kampfner, a political commentator, reported at the time that Mr Blair, together with Sir David Manning, had told the President that 'Britain would support him come what may'. To maximize support, however, they should try to build a large coalition, preferably through the United Nations.[20]

Certainly, in subserviently following the Bush administration into the war, the Prime minister faced two obstacles not as evident or as marked as in the United States. The first was the need to positively sway public opinion in favour of the war. Public opinion in the United Kingdom has been consistently opposed to the war. The second was the related need to establish a legal basis for the war. That legal basis was to prove elusive. These two needs undoubtedly underpinned the Prime Minister's actions, certainly in respect of the particular matters which I propose to examine below.

A judicial approach

In examining the following matters, I have sought to adhere to a judicial approach and judicial discipline. Having been a barrister for nigh on 32 years and a senior judge for 11 years, I am familiar with that approach. My appreciation that this approach is necessary reflects the seriousness of the charges that can be made against Mr Blair. The discipline inherent in the approach provides a safeguard against unjust or intemperate condemnation.

Judicial caution before attributing mendaciousness is well-established. Fraud is not to be lightly alleged nor lightly found. I have, therefore, consciously drawn back from reaching conclusions which might be said to contain an element of speculation. The famous – or infamous – 'judicial hunch' has no place in an inquiry of this kind. Hence, I believe that the conclusions I have reached are findings which would be considered respectable in a court of law.

---

19 Gaby Hinsliff, 'Blair in firing line on Iraq leak', *The Observer*, 19 September, 2004, at 4; Sands, *Lawless World*, supra n 13, pp 182-183.

20 John Kampfner, *Blair's Wars* (Free Press, 2003) p 168. In evidence to the Foreign Affairs Committee Clare Short has subsequently testified that 'senior people' had told her that Tony Blair had committed the country to war in the spring of 2002; Foreign Affairs Committee, evidence, 17 June 2003.

Furthermore, I am not unaware that the more severe the condemnation of Mr Blair, the more likely it is that one's analysis will be viewed as a polemic. But that concern cannot absolve one from following the facts to their proper conclusion. The temptation, often evident in judicial adjudication, to avoid the harsher finding and hold that Mr Blair was only reckless about the truth must bow to the evidence.

Then, I was conscious that my material was not hard evidence tested in cross examination. The information in books and articles is as yet incomplete and includes the authors' opinions. I considered that I could guard against this disadvantage by relying upon the factual data only, and I have at times spent as much time among the authors' footnotes as I have in his or her text.

Finally, I have been appreciative of the need to allow politicians a reasonable latitude. After all, politics is politics, and some are cynical enough to say that all or most politicians will at times, and possibly more than once, lie to their constituents. In judging them, they must be allowed the latitude to be scallywags but not rogues. But I proffer my judgment of Mr Blair confident that the level of his mendaciousness falls well outside any reasonable, or even generous, latitude.

Nonetheless, adopting a judicial approach and judicial discipline in examining the following matters does not mean that this work is in the nature of a legal judgment. It does not assume that style. Moreover, I must acknowledge that no effort is made to establish an assumption that permeates the paper. That assumption is the notion that neo-conservative policies are likely to reflect ideological thinking and consequently tend to be over-zealous, unrealistic, simplistic and single-minded. In the United Kingdom, such thinking has had minimal, or even negative, domestic appeal to the electorate. But my readiness to, in effect, take judicial notice of that perception will not satisfy some. Even if this perception of neo-conservative thinking is discounted, however, the evidence of Mr Blair's manipulation and deception remains compelling.

The matters which I propose to examine raise two broad questions which I cannot fully explore in this paper. The first question is: how can the political process be improved to better contain the excesses of executive power, particularly the far-reaching power of the Prime Minister in relation to foreign policy, and hold those responsible for the excesses accountable? The second question is: how assertive should the judiciary be in protecting human rights and civil liberties having regard to the reality of the political process? Both these questions are of paramount importance in determining the effectiveness and integrity of the political process and implementing the fundamental values of democracy.

In undertaking the following examination, I have not sought to conceal my personal belief that the decision to invade Iraq was a predictable mistake. But it is not necessary to be of that view to be disturbed at the manipulation and deception which took place leading up to the war. Indeed, the question of Mr Blair's culpability can be sensibly separated from the question whether the war was justified, including any claim that it was the execution of the war or post-war strategy that has been responsible for the subsequent calamity in that country.

Irrespective whether the war was justified or not, Mr Blair's behaviour in pursuing and prosecuting the war remains exactly the same. It deserved, and deserves, the same response from supporters and opponents of the war alike.

I turn now to the first matter that I consider demonstrates the lack of probity in Tony Blair's preparation for, and prosecution of, the war against Iraq.[21]

(1) From potentiality to actuality

I first want to examine the shift from the claim that Iraq had the *potential* to process weapons of mass destruction to the claim that Iraq *actually* possessed weapons of mass destruction. The shift was sudden, and has never been fully explained.

The narrative can begin in the early months of 2001. At this time Iraq was believed to pose a potential, rather than an actual, threat to peace and security. Tony Blair's belief then was that the menace presented by Saddam Hussein could be contained. He proclaimed that Iraq would seek to develop weapons of mass destruction 'given the chance'.[22] He told one newspaper, for example, that Iraq 'was still trying to acquire' a weapons of mass destruction capability.[23]

This assessment of the potentiality rather than the actuality of the threat posed by Iraq's weapons of mass destruction accorded with the analysis of the British intelligence agencies. The view of the Joint Intelligence Committee (JIC), the chief conduit of intelligence material for the Government, was that, while Iraq had 'increased the pace and scope' of its missile research and development programmes, it was probably in possession of only a handful of ageing Scud-derived missiles with 'little accuracy'.[24] While accepting that there were 'grounds for concern', officials pointed out that the intelligence was 'limited', 'patchy', and 'unclear'.[25]

A similar picture was also being presented by the United States intelligence agencies. Their conclusion was that Iraq did not as yet have any 'weaponised material'.[26] It was not as though Mr Blair had not been warned of the chicanery in Washington. A leaked memorandum records that Sir Richard Dearlove, the Chief of MI6, told a meeting of Mr Blair and top officials on 23 July 2002, that 'Bush wanted to remove Saddam, through military action, justified by the conjunction of terrorism and WMD. But the intelligence and facts were being fixed around the policy'.[27] Richard Dearlove's perception is confirmed by Tyler Drumheller, the former Chief of the CIA in Europe. Referring to the fact that the White House had dismissed the intelligence validated by the CIA in the run up to the war that Iraq

---

21 In carrying out this examination, I have obtained considerable assistance from two outstanding books; Steven Kettell, *Dirty Politics: New Labour, British Democracy and the Invasion of Iraq*, supra n 2, and Philippe Sands QC, *Lawless World: The whistle-blowing account of how Bush and Blair are taking the law into their own hands,* supra n 13.

22 Joint Press Conference at Camp David, 23 February, 2001.

23 Tony Blair, *The Observer*, 14 October, 2001.

24 Lord Butler, *Review of Intelligence on Weapons of Mass Destruction*, July 2004, paras. 218-288.

25 Ibid.

26 United States Senate Select Committee on Intelligence, *Report on the U.S. Intelligence Community's Prewar Intelligence Assessments on Iraq*, July 2004, 144-145; and see Bob Woodward, *Plan of Attack* (Simon & Schuster, London, 2004) p 194.

27 *Sunday Times*, 1 May, 2005. See also Ricks in *Fiasco*, supra n 2, at p 39.

had no weapons of mass destruction, he said: 'The policy was set. The war in Iraq was coming. And they [the Bush administration] were looking for intelligence to fit into the policy, to justify the policy'.[28] Similarly, a former director of the strategic proliferation and military affairs office in the United States Department of State, Greg Thielmann, was to say in July 2003, that, 'this administration has had a faith-based intelligence attitude [in] its top-down use of intelligence: we know the answers, give us the intelligence to support those answers'.[29]

Yet, in a matter of months only the potentiality became the actuality. Tony Blair now asserted that Iraq actually possessed weapons of mass destruction. This assertion was repeated incessantly and was part of a concerted public relations campaign to convince the public that Saddam Hussein posed a current threat to the peace and security of the world. Mr Blair was unequivocal; he now described Iraq's claims to have no weapons of mass destruction as a blatant lie professing to 'know' that Iraq was developing weapons of mass destruction;[30] he told the House of Commons that Iraq was developing weapons of mass destruction which posed a threat 'not just to the region, but to the wider world';[31] he told journalists that Iraq had 'actually acquired weapons of mass destruction' and that the threat was 'not in any doubt at all';[32] he told the American television channel, NBC, that Iraq was in possession of 'major amounts of chemical and biological weapons';[33] and Iraq, he said, was spending around £3 billion of illicit funds a year on weapons of mass destruction programmes.[34]

In his book, *Disarming Iraq: The Search for Weapons on Mass Destruction*,[35] Hans Blix notes how Tony Blair's mindset had changed. He was now asserting that weapons of mass destruction did exist and could be used almost immediately. Blix quotes Mr Blair's statement to the NBC[36] adding his own emphasis. The Prime Minister stated: 'We know he [Saddam Hussein] has *major amounts of chemical and biological weapons*. We know that he's tried to acquire nuclear capability'.[37] Hans Blix repeatedly refused to condone these flat assertions.[38]

One would expect this sudden and positive shift from potentiality to actuality, from possibility to certainty, to reflect further and more positive intelligence. It did not. At the time intelligence in both the United Kingdom and the United States remained heavily qualified and non-committal. The JIC's assessment of Iraq's weapons of mass destruction capacity remained markedly negative.[39] The

28 Blumenthal, *How Bush Rules*, supra n 1, p 402.
29 Quoted in Hans Blix, *Disarming Iraq: The Search for Weapons of Mass Destruction* (Bloomsbury, 2004), p 263.
30 Tony Blair, press conference, 6 April 2002.
31 Tony Blair, statement to the House of Commons, 10 April, 2002
32 Joint press conference with Dick Cheney, 11 March, 2002.
33 NBC, 4 April, 2002.
34 Tony Blair, speech to the TUC Conference, 10 September, 2002.
35 Supra n 29, at pp 60-61.
36 See n 33 above.
37 Supra n 29, at p 61.
38 Ibid, at p 111.
39 Butler Report, supra n 24, paras. 327, 331, 466. 573-578.

Committee noted that intelligence on the subject was 'poor' and that it was founded on 'sporadic and patchy' information. There was, it said, very little evidence to suggest that any chemical, biological, or nuclear weapons' programmes were currently being pursued.[40]

The conclusion is inescapable that the campaign led by Mr Blair was founded on a pretence. Nevertheless, Mr Blair was to assert, then and later, that the claim Iraq possessed weapons of mass destruction was based on intelligence. But the intelligence, as I have indicated, conferred no such basis. Peter Ricketts, the Political Director of the Foreign Office correctly analysed the position when outlining his concerns to Jack Straw, the Foreign Secretary. He observed that what had changed was not the pace of Saddam Hussein's weapons of mass destruction programmes, but the Government's tolerance of them post September 11.[41] But a different level of tolerance cannot, of itself, convert the potential for Iraq to possess weapons of mass destruction into the actuality that it possessed those weapons.

Many persons who witnessed Mr Blair's repeated claims on television that Iraq possessed weapons of mass destruction, persisted with long after the invasion had begun, will find it difficult to conclude that he did not genuinely believe that such weapons would be found. I share that difficulty. Why would the Prime Minister persist with a claim if he knew that the claim would eventually be shown to be false? Furthermore, as Hans Blix has noted, the United States leadership appears to have been convinced that Iraq had an ample supply of unconventional weapons in that protective suits were distributed to their troops and donned repeatedly in the first part of the military campaign. This prudence, he observes, was understandable. What Blix finds amazing, however, is that several hundred million dollars had been budgeted for the destruction of any weapons of mass destruction that might be found.[42] Clearly, the Bush administration spoke with the voice of infallibility. At some point, Tony Blair appears to have bought into this 'faith-based intelligence'.

For that reason I do not consider that, however inept his endorsement of this faith-based intelligence might have been, it is possible to charge the Prime Minister with deliberately lying in continuing to assert that weapons of mass destruction existed in Iraq. When Hans Blix put it to him that it would be absurd if 250,000 troops were to invade Iraq and find very little, the Prime Minister responded that the 'intelligence' was clear that Saddam had reconstituted his weapons of mass destruction programmes. He was apparently unperturbed that Hans Blix's faith in the intelligence has been shaken by the fact that not one of the sites given to him by the intelligence agencies in the United States as sites housing, or suspected of housing, weapons of mass destruction were found to harbour those weapons.[43]

---

40 Ibid.

41 Memorandum, Ricketts to Straw, 22 March 2002.

42 Supra n 29, at pp 255-256.

43 Supra n 29, at pp 194 and 93.

Rather, the focus must be more narrowly drawn, I believe that the Prime Minister's culpability lies in the fact that he moved from saying one day that Iraq had the potential to develop weapons of mass destruction to saying, in effect, the next day, that Iraq actually possessed those weapons when there was no basis for that change in the intelligence emanating from the intelligence services. At this time, of course, there is no suggestion that the intelligence had been influenced or manipulated by political pressure. Even if the shift from potentiality to actuality was in response to the direction or line being taken in Washington, Mr Blair had to know that the intelligence as it then stood simply did not support the claim.[44] While, therefore, Mr Blair may in time have come to believe that Saddam Hussein possessed weapons of mass destruction, he could not initially have believed that to be the case in the absence of hard intelligence to that effect. At the very least, it was duplicitous to assert as an established fact that Iraq actually possessed weapons of mass destruction without at the same time disclosing that the intelligence was far from unequivocal.

One possible explanation is that, spurred by the need to convert public opinion in favour of the war and to establish a basis for justifying the legality of the invasion of Iraq, the Prime Minister was quick to resort to a lie as part of the intensive public relations campaign which he headed. Necessity was the mother to the lie. Perhaps with the passage of time and the repetition of the claim on an almost daily basis he came to believe the lie. This phenomenon is not unknown in the world of debating, and Mr Blair is undeniably a master debater. Another possibility is that the Prime Minister was convinced that Saddam Hussein would not have destroyed all the weapons of mass destruction in existence at the end of the first Gulf war as required by resolution 687 of the United Nations.[45] Thus, although Iraq lacked the missiles to effectively deploy the lethal weapons, some weapons of mass destruction would be found. On this basis the claim that Iraq possessed weapons of mass destruction, and the threat posed by Iraq under Saddam Hussein, could be exaggerated without significant adverse political fallout.

Whether either of these possibilities, or any other possibility, emerges to explain Mr Blair's motivation can, however, be left to the future. For the present, one can accept Hans Blix's conclusion that Tony Blair's (and the Bush administration's) approach demonstrated a 'deficit of critical thinking'.[46] The contention that Iraq possessed weapons of mass destruction was 'simply wrong' and could have been avoided with a 'moderate dose of prudence'. Hans Blix concludes that it would not have taken much critical thinking on the part of Mr Bush and Mr Blair, or on the part of their close advisers, to preclude statements

---

44 Blumenthal, *How Bush Rules*, supra n 1, p 31, suggests the opposite. He claims that Bush originally came to Blair determined to go to war in Iraq, but without a strategy, and that it was Blair who instructed him that the *casus belli* was Saddam Hussein's weapons of mass destruction.

45 Security Council resolution, 3 April, 1991. Adopting a ceasefire, the resolution imposed obligations on Iraq to disarm and to destroy all chemical and biological weapons of mass destruction. It also established the system of United Nations inspections, which continued until 1998, to ensure Iraq's compliance.

46 Supra n 29, at p 263.

being made which misled the public.[47]

While agreeing that Tony Blair approached the intelligence with a surprising lack of prudence and critical thinking, however, I am not prepared to absolve Mr Blair of more severe censure. His subsequent sincere adoption and assertion of the claim that Saddam Hussein possessed weapons of mass destruction does not eradicate his original guile. I remain satisfied that the original decision to convert the claim that Iraq had the potential to develop weapons of mass destruction to an unqualified assertion that Iraq actually possessed weapons of mass destruction can only have been a deliberate deception.

(2) The first dossier

There were three dossiers. I propose to focus on the first.[48] Focusing on the first dossier, however, does not mean that the veracity of the second and third dossiers is to be accepted. More than half the second dossier, it will be recalled, had been directly copied, without attribution to the author and replete with grammatical and typographical errors, from an article posted on the internet. The article derived from a 12 year old PhD thesis[49] and, even then, sections were doctored to make it appear as if it were the work of the intelligence agencies. Not unexpectedly, the author claimed that his work had been distorted. Mr Blair's defence; the article had been amended 'to reflect the actual situation in Iraq'![50] The third dossier issued shortly afterwards sought to focus on Iraq's human rights abuses instead of its military capabilities. Until uncovered through the media, it was not widely known that the document was the work of Alastair Campbell, the Government's Director of Communications, and not the intelligence services. Amnesty International condemned the dossier for being 'opportunistic and selective.'[51]

The first dossier was critical in that it was intended to convince the British public that Iraq possessed weapons of mass destruction and was therefore an immediate threat. Peter Ricketts presented Mr Blair's dilemma in stark terms:

> To get public and Parliamentary support for military options we have to be convincing that the threat is so serious/imminent that it is worth sending our troops to die for.[52]

To this end, a dossier was eventually constructed which conveyed a significantly different picture from that presented by the intelligence agencies. The intelligence and security services had been for some time expressing deep concern about the pressure placed on them by their political masters and the use to which the secret information would be put. According to a columnist who consistently saw the folly of a war which would ignite Islamist extremism and convert Iraq into an almost inexhaustible

47 Ibid, at p 260.

48 *Iraq's Weapons of Mass Destruction: The Assessment of the British Government*, 24 September, 2002 (the first dossier).

49 Ibrahim al-Marashi, 'Iraq's Security & Intelligence Network: A Guide & Analysis', published in *Middle East Review of International Affairs*, September, 2002.

50 Kettell, *Dirty Politics*, supra n 2, p 89.

51 Ibid, p 85.

52 Memorandum, Ricketts to Straw, supra n 41.

recruiting ground for further terrorists, the intelligence services never wanted an intelligence dossier published. Initially, they managed to thwart the idea by telling Downing Street that there was nothing new to say. But political pressure prevailed.[53]

The dossier, however, was not accepted without some protest. Dr Bryan Jones, the head of the Nuclear, Chemical and Biological Warfare Division of the Defence Intelligence Staff condemned the claims being made about Iraq's possession of weapons of mass destruction as 'far too strong'. He maintained that Mr Blair's claim to 'know' that Iraq was in possession of such weapons 'was simply not true'.[54] And as John Morrison, former Deputy Chief of Britain's Defence Intelligence Staff, later somewhat colloquially reported, the Prime Minister's promulgations were greeted throughout Whitehall with a 'collective raspberry.'[55]

Mr Blair appointed Alastair Campbell in charge of a team to supervise the dossier 'from a presentational point of view' and to 'make recommendations and suggestions to the [head of intelligence] as to how it could be improved.'[56] Mr Campbell was answerable to Tony Blair alone. Moreover, in a dubious utilization of the Crown's prerogative powers, Mr Blair had conferred on Mr Campbell the far-reaching power to issue direct orders to civil servants.[57] I will not traverse in full the political manipulation that then transpired. Suffice it to say, early drafts were rejected as being insufficiently strong. Mr Campbell, himself, noted that the earlier dossier was 'not terribly good'.[58]

A brief indication of the climate in which the dossier was produced is evident from the comments of Jonathan Powell, the Prime Minister's Chief of Staff. Mr Powell sent an email to Alastair Campbell and John Scarlett, who chaired the JIC, reminding them of the need for the kind of headline they wished to see in the *Evening Standard* following publication of the dossier.[59] He claimed that the description of Saddam's willingness to use weapons of mass destruction 'if he believes his regime is under threat' was 'a bit of a problem'. The problem he foresaw with this statement was that it would support the argument Iraq did not in fact pose a current threat and that 'we [Great Britain] will only create one if we attack him'. He suggested that the paragraph should be deleted.[60] By the time the dossier had been published, and unknown to the members of the JIC, the paragraph had been deleted. Other key statements which were struck out were the section admitting that the Government's knowledge of the Iraq situation was 'partial' and that Saddam would only use weapons of mass destruction 'to protect his power and eventually to project it when he feels strong enough to do so'.[61] So

53 Richard Norton-Taylor, *The Guardian*, 28 June 2003.

54 Kettell, *Dirty Politics*, supra n 2, p 73.

55 Ibid.

56 Ibid, p 72.

57 Ibid, pp 21-22.

58 Ibid, p 69.

59 Email, Powell to Campbell and Scarlett, 19 September, 2002.

60 Ibid

61 Kettell, *Dirty Politics*, supra n 2, pp 74-75. Kettell also records that the title was changed from 'Iraq's Programme for Weapons of Mass Destruction' to the more assertive 'Iraq's Weapons of Mass Destruction'.

too, a statement by Hans Blix to the Associated Press a month before the dossier was published saying that he could not confirm that Bagdad had weapons of mass destruction was excised from the document.[62]

There were many other respects in which the dossier as finally published bore little resemblance to the heavily qualified intelligence that pre-dated this manipulation. What Robert Fisk calls 'weasel' words litter the document; such words as 'almost certainly', 'appears', 'probably' and 'if'.[63] To claim, as Mr Blair had to claim, that the dossier established a threat so serious and imminent that it was 'worth sending … troops to die for' was nothing short of an obscenity. The public were misled. As Hans Blix so pungently observed, the Government 'put exclamation marks where there had been question marks'.[64]

A similar point was made by the late Robin Cook who pointed to the clear evidence from both the Hutton Inquiry and the Butler Report that Parliament had been 'misled into voting for war on the basis of unreliable sources and overheated analysis.'[65]

Mr Blair's responsibility for this duplicity is not just the responsibility of the Minister in charge. He was closely involved in the preparation of the dossier. As indicated, Alastair Campbell was answerable to him and no one else. At the very least, one is forced to accept the verdict of Hans Blix; Mr Blair did not act in 'good faith'.[66]

Needless to say, Mr Blair has hotly denied fabricating the intelligence. The idea, he repeated, that he 'made our intelligence agencies invent some piece of evidence' was 'completely absurd'. No one, he claimed, had sought to 'insert' concocted information into the dossier in order to strengthen the case for war.[67] But this denial misses the point. The point is not that Mr Blair and his close advisers actually 'invented' intelligence information, but rather that intelligence information was misused in the course of constructing the dossier. The real strengthening of the dossier came, not through the insertion of information, as in the clever use of 'weasel' words and the wholesale removal of caveats and uncertainties from the assessments of the JIC.

Tony Blair's culpability rests in the fact that he sanctioned the strengthening process by which the distortion occurred, and then endorsed and represented that distorted material to Cabinet, Parliament and the people as genuine intelligence. It has to be said that people have been found liable for fraudulent misrepresentation on less evidence than this.

(3) The 45 minute claim

A specific item in the September dossier deserves particular mention. It was one of the few pieces of new information to be included in the dossier, and one which

62 Robert Fisk, *The Great War for Civilisation: the Conquest of the Middle East* (Fourth Estate, London, 2005) pp 114-115.

63 Ibid, p 115.

64 Hans Blix, *HardTalk*, BBC, 15 July, 2004.

65 Robin Cook, 'Britain's worst intelligence failure, and Lord Butler says no one is to blame', *The Independent*, 15 July, 2004; and *BBC Radio*, 4 August, 2004.

66 See above, n 64.

67 E.g. Tony Blair, press comments on *Sky News*, 1 June, 2003, and press conference in Warsaw, 30 May, 2003.

undoubtedly had a dramatic impact on public opinion. This item was the claim that Iraq's possession of weapons of mass destruction had been 'established beyond doubt', that these 'could be activated within 45 minutes' (repeated no less than four times) and that Iraq had 'existing and active military plans' for their use.[68] Undoubtedly aware of its impact on public opinion, Tony Blair repeatedly stressed this 'intelligence'. He repeated it in the House of Commons.[69] It was given dramatic headlines in the daily press. But the claim was false.

The secret and limited information on which the claim was based was so unreliable that it was withdrawn by the intelligence services the following July.[70] But even at the time, the inclusion of the claim in the dossier was criticized by the Foreign Affairs Committee and the Intelligence and Security Committee.[71] Its inclusion was later criticized in the Butler Report.[72] Worse still, the 'intelligence' referred to battlefield chemical weapons, and not long-range missiles. Mr Blair purported to have been unaware of the unreliability of the so-called intelligence and the fact that the claim referred to battlefield munitions and not weapons of mass destruction prior to launching the war.[73]

Steven Kettell argues that one is led inexorably to one of only two possible conclusions. The first is that the Prime Minister wilfully and knowingly misled Parliament and the British public by fostering the impression that Iraq was capable of launching a full scale attack using weapons of mass destruction within three quarters of an hour. The second is that the Prime Minister did not think to inquire into, and likewise nobody thought to inform him about, the specific nature of the intelligence.[74]

As tempting as it is to adopt the less iniquitous of these two possibilities, I am unable to do so. The evidence, I believe, points to a deliberate deception on the part of Mr Blair.

Consider, first, the persons who were fully aware that the intelligence related to battlefield munitions and not weapons of mass destruction. All the intelligence analysts knew. In particular, the members of the JIC were fully aware of the limited scope of the claim. John Scarlett, the head of the JIC, and Richard Dearlove, Chief of MI6, both had access to the Prime Minister. Others who have been recorded as being aware of the distinction included Jack Straw, the Foreign Secretary, Geoff Hoon, the Minister of Defence, Alastair Campbell and Robin Cook.[75]

It beggars belief that Tony Blair alone could have been under a genuine misapprehension as to the nature of the 'intelligence'. Coincidences do occur, but it would be an amazing coincidence if, of all those who were privy to this

---

68 The first dossier, supra n 48, p 17.
69 Tony Blair, statement to the House of Commons, 24 September, 2002.
70 Marie Woolf, 'The 45-minute claim was false' *The Independent*, 13 October, 2004.
71 Kettell, *Dirty Politics*, supra n 2, p 77.
72 Butler Report, supra n 24, para. 511.
73 Tony Blair, statement in the House of Commons, 20 July, 2004.
74 Kettell, *Dirty Politics*, supra n 2, pp 77-78.
75 Ibid, p 77.

information, the one person who misunderstood it was the Prime Minister.

Further, it also strains credibility to believe that, with the JIC and a number of others, including ministerial colleagues, being aware of the true scope of the 'intelligence', Mr Blair was not informed that he was misrepresenting the 45 minute claim. Yet, Mr Blair repeated the wrong 'intelligence' over a period of months. He continued to repeat the claim even after it had been withdrawn from the dossier on the ground of its unreliability.[76] It is difficult, if not impossible, to believe that in all that time no one on the JIC or in the intelligence services thought to tell the Prime Minister of his error. It is also difficult, if not impossible, to believe that not one of them would have penned a memorandum to the Prime Minister, or the Prime Minister's Office, correcting the misrepresentation, a misrepresentation which they were fully aware the Prime Minister was repeating to Parliament and propagating to the people. Equally, it is difficult, if not impossible, to believe that those of his colleagues who were aware of the true scope of the claim, such as Jack Straw and Geoff Hoon, did not draw their leader's attention to his continuing critical misstatement.

I am drawn to the conclusion that, if Mr Blair were to be cross-examined on this issue by a reasonably competent counsel, he could not emerge with his credibility intact.

I believe that the 45 minute claim had to be a knowing lie.

(4) The Attorney-General's advice on the legality of the war

The story of the Attorney-General's advice to the Prime Minister on the legality of the war is an astonishing saga. In fact, there were two opinions given by the Attorney-General, one on the 7 March and the other, ten days later, on the 17 March. Although proximate it time, they are clearly inconsistent.

From the outset, the Attorney-General had expressed considerable unease as to the legality of the pending war.[77] The Foreign Office was even more forthright in its repeated view that there was no valid legal basis for the war.[78] A number of possible grounds were excluded. It was generally agreed that the Bush doctrine of pre-emption was not 'recognized in international law'; that a war to achieve a regime change could 'not be the objective of any military action'; that attacking Iraq on humanitarian grounds was not 'an appropriate basis for action …'; and that the use of force could only be authorized by an entirely new resolution of the United Nations.[79]

Mr Blair deferred obtaining formal advice as to the legality of the war until the latest possible moment. He told the Cabinet, '[t]he time to debate the legal base for our action should be when we take that action.'[80] Not only does such a notion defy both custom and good sense, but the Ministerial Code of Conduct requires

76 Mr Blair purported not to know that the claim had been withdrawn; Kettell, *Dirty Politics*, supra n 2, p 152.

77 Sands, *Lawless World*, supra n 13, pp 183-184.

78 'Iraq: Legal Background', Foreign and Commonwealth Office briefing paper, 8 March, 2002.

79 See Memorandum from the Attorney-General to the Prime Minister, 7 March, 2003.

80 Robin Cook, *The Point of Departure: Diaries from the Front Bench* (Pocket Books, 2004) p 135.

the Attorney-General to be 'consulted in good time before the Government is committed to critical decisions involving legal considerations'.[81]

The Attorney-General's formal advice was given on 7 March in a 13 page memorandum.[82] This memorandum remained a tightly guarded secret until part of it was leaked 18 months later just before the General Election in 2005. The Prime Minister, in an exercise of damage control, published the full contents of the memorandum one week before polling day.

As the advice given on 17 March, however, was the first advice made public it is convenient to deal with it first. In a short memorandum prepared in answer to a question in the House of Lords and taking up little more than one side of A4 paper, the Attorney-General relied upon what is called the revival argument, that is, the authority to use force contained in resolutions relating to the first Gulf war were revived if Iraq was in material breach of those resolutions.[83] As Philippe Sands QC has written: 'The argument is well spun and could, at a pinch, win the prize for the most plausible response to the question: what is the best possible argument to justify the use of force in Iraq in March 2003?'[84]

I will not pursue the detail of this argument but there can be little doubt that it is specious. Few states and virtually no established international lawyers accept it as valid. Nor did the Foreign Office's legal advisers. Indeed, the Office's Deputy Legal Adviser, Elizabeth Wilmshurst, sought early retirement or resignation in protest. She wrote that she could not 'agree that it is lawful to use force without a second Security Council resolution'. With courage to match her conscience, she added, 'I cannot in conscience go along with advice within the Office or to the public or Parliament, which asserts the legitimacy of military action without such a resolution, particularly since an unlawful use of force on such a scale amounts to the crime of aggression; nor can I agree with such action in circumstances which are so detrimental to the international order and the rule of law'.[85]

Having studied the Attorney-General's argument, I can confirm that it is fanciful on a number of grounds. Apart from resolution 1441, the resolutions related to the first Gulf war. They had effectively become otiose by the ceasefire in 1991. Then, in resolution 1441 the Security Council determined that Iraq had been and remained in material breach of resolution 687 requiring Iraq to eliminate its weapons of mass destruction. It gave Iraq a 'final opportunity to comply with its disarmament obligations' and warned the country that it would face 'serious consequences' if it did not. The Security Council required a dossier listing Iraq's weapons of mass destruction within 30 days and stated that failure to cooperate

81 *Ministerial Code: A Code of Conduct and Guidance on Procedures for Ministers*, Cabinet Office, July 2001, para. 22.

82 The Attorney-General's advice is conveniently appended to Sands, *Lawless World*, supra n 13, Appendix X, p 328. The advice of 17 March is appended as Appendix XI, 343.

83 Ibid, Appendix XI, 343-344.

84 Sands, *Lawless World*, supra n 13, p 189.

85 Elizabeth Wilmshurst resigned the day following the Attorney-General's advice. See V. Dodd, 'Iraq war illegal, says FO adviser who quit', *The Guardian*, 14 June 2004. See also http://www.guardian.co.uk/Iraq/Story/0,,1238122,00.html

fully with the weapons' inspectors would constitute a material breach of its obligations. Should that happen, the Council would then convene immediately 'in order to consider the situation'.[86]

On the face of it, the resolution anticipated that the Security Council would make an assessment of the situation in the event of an adverse report from Hans Blix, as the head of the United Nations Monitoring, Verification and Inspection Commission, or Mohammed ElBaradei, as the Director General of the International Atomic Energy Agency. There can be little doubt that, as the resolution is worded and having regard to its context, any determination that there had been a material breach was one for the Security Council to make.

How, then, in the absence of this determination, was this pre-condition to the Attorney-General's advice given on the 17 March satisfied? The Prime Minister simply informed the Attorney-General that it was his 'unequivocal view' that Iraq was, indeed, 'in further material breach' of its obligations to the United Nations.[87] And that was it. Although the Attorney-General advised that legal authority would be contingent on the existence of weapons of mass destruction and that 'strong factual grounds' and 'hard evidence' would be required, no process or procedure was suggested for resolving this prerequisite.[88] Mr Blair has never explained how he came to his conclusion and no supporting evidence has been provided. The best evidence, the reports of Hans Blix and Mohammed ElBaradie, although evidence to the contrary, was apparently ignored. Nor was any step taken to ascertain the current views of the JIC. The Prime Minister's word alone sufficed to 'revive' the authority of the earlier resolutions. In the result, with the Attorney-General's advice in hand, Cabinet and Parliament accepted that the war was legal.[89]

One can test the soundness – or unsoundness – of the Attorney-General's advice by positing the same question in a different context; if he had been asked whether, say, Iran could unilaterally decide that Iraq was in breach of its obligations to the United Nations and lawfully use force to remove Saddam Hussein from power, would he have given the same answer? Of course, he would not, and if he had, it is not overstepping the mark to suggest that his advice would have been viewed with disbelief. If it had been further suggested that the decision whether Iraq was in material breach of its obligations to the United Nations was one that the President of Iran could simply dictate, his advice would have been met with derision.

The normally circumspect Secretary-General of the United Nations, Kofi Annan, was later prompted to take the unexpected step of emphatically stating that the Iraq war was illegal.[90]

Throughout this time, Cabinet, Ministers, Members of Parliament and the

---

86 Resolution 1441, adopted 8 November, 2002.

87 Kettell, *Dirty Politics*, supra n 2, p 102.

88 Butler Report, supra n 24, paras. 379, 383-386. C Short, *An Honourable Deception? New Labour, Iraq, and the Misuse of Power* (Free Press, London, 2004).

89 But Tony Blair's advisers must have had some misgivings. They took steps to put together a legal team to prepare for the possibility of international litigation. See Sands, *Lawless World*, supra n 13, p 197.

90 Statement, September, 2004. http://news.bbc.co.uk/2/hi/middle_east/3661134.stm

public remained unaware of the contents of the Attorney-General's earlier opinion of 7 March.[91] Questioned about it, the Prime Minister managed to convey that the advice given on the 17 March was a summary or précis of the Attorney-General's formal opinion given ten days earlier. It was, he said, a 'fair summary'.[92] The suggestion 'that the legal opinion of the Attorney-General was different from the Attorney-General's statement to the House', he proclaimed, 'is patently absurd'.[93]

When the Prime Minister's hand was eventually forced and the formal advice of 7 March was published, it was at once apparent that the 17 March advice was inconsistent with the earlier opinion. The caution, doubts and caveats in the formal opinion were absent and the inconsistencies were manifest. On 7 March the Attorney-General had advised the Prime Minister that, while a 'reasonable case' could be made that resolution 1441 was 'capable in principle' of reviving the authorization to invade Iraq, he could not be 'confident' that the argument would succeed in a court of law.[94] In other words, as any lawyer will recognize, the Attorney-General was saying that, while the Prime Minister could choose to run with the revival argument, he should not expect it to survive a legal challenge.

In the formal opinion of 7 March the Attorney-General had also advised that the United Kingdom had consistently taken the view that it was for the Security Council to assess whether any breach of the earlier resolutions had occurred. He maintained: 'On the United Kingdom view of the revival argument only the Council can decide if a violation is sufficiently serious to revive the authorization to use force'.[95] As we have seen, ten days later this requirement had been varied to permit the Prime Minister alone to decide that key question.

It is legitimate to ask what had happened to the perceived threat from Iraq in this ten day period to cause the Attorney-General to so dramatically revise his advice. Some new argument or development or further intelligence could be expected. But there was none. No new and previously unknown evidence of weapons of mass destruction emerged. To the contrary, Hans Blix provided his third and final report in which he said that, although Iraqi co-operation was not wholehearted, it was accelerating.[96] Nor had any new argument been advanced. All

91 In The Sixth Sir David Williams Lecture, 'the Rule of Law' (publication pending) Lord Bingham of Cornhill, the senior Law Lord, recently questioned whether the ordinary rules of client professional privilege, appropriate enough in other circumstances, should apply to a law officer's opinion on the lawfulness of war. He expressed the view that it is not unrealistic to regard the public, those who are to fight and perhaps die, rather than the government, as the client. An opinion on the lawfulness of war, being the ultimate exercise of sovereign power involving the whole people was, he thought, quite different from situations where the ordinary rules of client professional privilege would apply. He added that the case for full contemporaneous disclosure would seem to be even stronger when the Attorney-General is a peer and not susceptible to direct questioning in the Chamber.

92 Kettell, *Dirty Politics*, supra n 2, p 163.

93 Tony Blair, 9 March 2005. For a decisive refutation of this claim, see Sands, *Lawless World*, supra n 13, Chapter 12, 'This Wretched Legal Advice', p 258 *et seq*.

94 Sands, *Lawless World*, supra n 13, p 268.

95 Kettell, *Dirty Politics*, supra n 2, p 98.

96 Hans Blix's third and final report was also provided on 7 March. Mr Blix denied that it could be said Iraq was in substantial non-compliance and claimed that there was no evidence to the contrary; see *Financial Times*, 28 April, 2005. The increasing co-operation of Iraq is traced by Hans Blix in *Disarming Iraq*, supra n 29, at pp 148-149, 178 and 215.

the legal issues had been fully aired in the formal opinion given on 7 March.

I cannot accept that the equivocations, reservations and caveats stipulated in the advice of 7 March could, in the absence of an intervening event, dissolve so completely as to make way for such an unequivocal view as that expressed in the 17 March document. Nor can Lord Lester QC. The leading Queen's Counsel has had this to say:

> After being in the business for 40 years I cannot recall a single example where I have given firm advice of this kind and then changed my mind in this way except where there was some mistake or a client misled me, but otherwise it would be unheard of.[97]

One significant event, however, had occurred. Admiral Sir Michael Boyce, the Chief of Defence Staff, was not satisfied that a legal basis for the war had been established. He demanded more concrete assurances from the Prime Minister that the war would be legal. His concerns were transmitted to the Attorney-General through the Prime Minister.[98] The Attorney-General's second effort on 17 March was then provided and accepted by the Chief of Defence Staff.[99] Sir Michael Boyce was not the only senior military officer to express misgivings at the absence of a legal justification for the war. Chief of Staff, Sir Mike Jackson, is on record as having said: 'I spent a good deal of time recently in the Balkans making sure Milosevic was put behind bars. I have no intention of ending up in the next cell to him in the Hague'.[100]

One can only speculate what would have happened, if, just days before the invasion was to commence, the military had not got the unequivocal assurance it sought that the war was legal. The pressure on the Prime Minister must have been enormous.[101]

Reaction to the Attorney-General's about face is indicated by the fact that a group of fifty barristers, including four Queen's Counsel, complained to the Bar Council. They requested an investigation into the possibility that the Attorney-General's advice of 17 March did not reflect the contents of his formal opinion. The basis of the complaint were the provisions in the Bar's Code of Conduct requiring of a barrister independence, integrity and freedom from external pressure and a refusal to compromise professional standards to please a client. The Bar Council determined that it did not have jurisdiction to investigate the complaint.[102]

But I am here concerned with the Prime Minister's involvement. Obviously, many authors and commentators suspect that he manipulated the presentation of

97 'The Document and What it Means', reported in *The Guardian*, 28 April, 2005.

98 Sands, Lawless World, supra n 13, p 197.

99 *The Times*, 18 March, 2003.

100 R Norton-Taylor, 'Revealed – the rush to war', *The Guardian*, 23 February, 2005.

101 Legal validation for the war was also necessary to avoid the possible resignation of Cabinet Ministers if its legality were not verified. Similarly, the legal advice was necessary to maintain the support of back bench Members of Parliament who might vote against the war when the issue was bought before the House of Commons. See Sands, supra n 13, p 175.

102 Sands, *Lawless World*, supra n 13, p 376, n 36.

legal advice as he had manipulated the intelligence on weapons of mass destruction. Indeed, Clare Short, the Minister who ultimately resigned, has since openly charged the Prime Minister with bringing political pressure to bear on the Attorney-General.[103] But it must be acknowledged that there is no direct evidence of pressure or manipulation by the Prime Minister.

What is certain is that Mr Blair, who had repeatedly stated that Britain would only act within the bounds of international law,[104] knew of the significant differences in the two documents and that the uncertainties and reservations in the March 7 opinion had been removed from the 17 March document. Mr Blair must have known, particularly as a barrister, that this latter advice was not a 'fair summary' of the formal opinion. He must also have known that any suggestion the advice of 7 March had not been changed could not be described as 'patently absurd'. Mr Blair would also have known that the information being put before Cabinet was seriously incomplete and would give Ministers an incorrect understanding of the Attorney-General's advice. He must also have known that putting the Attorney-General's 17 March advice only before Cabinet was a breach of the Ministerial Code of Conduct which stipulates that full legal advice must be disclosed to Ministers whenever they are presented with a summarized version of the advice.[105]

In all, I am satisfied that the Prime Minister was duplicitous and that that duplicity was deliberate. This conclusion is serious. The Attorney-General advised in his formal 7 March opinion that the International Criminal Court at present has no jurisdiction over the crime of aggression and could therefore not entertain a case concerning the lawfulness of any military action.[106] He also correctly pointed out, however, that: 'Aggression is a crime under customary international law which automatically forms part of domestic law' and that 'it might therefore be argued that international aggression is a crime recognised by the common law which can be prosecuted in the UK courts'.[107] In this opinion, the Attorney-General was right. The House of Lords have subsequently held that the crime of aggression is established in customary international law and its core elements have been understood, at least since 1945, with sufficient clarity to permit the lawful prosecution (and, on conviction) punishment of those accused of this crime.[108]

---

103 Clare Short has also accused the Attorney-General of having succumbed to political pressure and of having 'misled the Cabinet' by failing to disclose his uncertainty and reservations about the legal situation. See Kettell, supra n 2, p 162.

104 Sands, *Lawless World*, supra n 13, p 175.

105 *Ministerial Code of Conduct*, supra n 81, para. 23. Paragraph 23 states: 'When advice from the law officer is included in correspondence between Ministers, or papers for the Cabinet or Ministerial Committees, the conclusions may if necessary be summarised but, if this is done, the complete text of the advice should be attached.'

106 Supra n 79, para. 33.

107 Ibid, para. 34.

108 *Regina* v *Jones (Margaret) and Others, Ayliffe and Others* v *Director of Public Prosecutions; Swain* v *Director of Public Prosecutions* [2006] UKHL 16. See esp Lord Bingham of Cornhill at paras. 10-19. Their Lordships went on to hold, as a matter of interpretation in the context of that particular case, that the crime of aggression was not a crime or offence within the meaning of s 3 of the Criminal Law Act, 1967.

As extreme as it sounds, it is difficult to resist the conclusion that, should he be prosecuted at a time when the plea of sovereign immunity is not available, Mr Blair would be found guilty of a war crime.

(5) Forgiving tolerance to torture.

I have included this heading because I believe that torture in all its forms is the ultimate denial of human rights. It denies a person's dignity and humanity. It is cruel and inhumane, and it is degrading to both the torturer and the tortured. It is illegal and contrary to international law, and alien to any sensible concept of civilization. Laws prohibiting torture protect us from our worst selves; from descending to the lowest depths of humanity.[109] Further, as is well documented, information gained by torture is notoriously unreliable.

Philippe Sands QC has provided a comprehensive account of the Bush administration's twisted dalliance with torture.[110] I do not propose to canvass what, by any objective standard, is a remarkable departure from the values that underlie democracy. My present concern is that Tony Blair has been indifferent, to the point of tolerance, of the use of torture against terrorist suspects. While frequently claiming to abhor torture, the outright condemnation expected has not been forthcoming.

Asked to comment on the outrages at Guantanamo Bay, for example, the Prime Minister acknowledged that it was an 'anomaly' but stressed that it is important to have an understanding of the huge amount of anger there is in America following September 11.[111] Referred to the fact that the United States was deporting or returning people to other countries where they would be tortured, he complained that people spent too little time in actually looking at the threat the United States and United Kingdom faces and how to deal with it.[112] The question will be asked by many, especially those sensitive to abuses of human rights, whether Mr Blair's proclaimed abhorrence of torture is lacking in substantive conviction.

There are, I believe, two main respects in which Mr Blair may be held accountable for adopting a too forgiving accommodation of torture.

The first relates to the United States' policy of extraordinary rendition. No sensible distinction can be drawn between administering torture to a person within a country and removing that person to another country to be tortured. As an unnamed United States official interviewed by the *Washington Post* said in 2002; 'We don't kick the [expletive] out of them. We send them to other countries so they can kick the [expletive] out of them'.[113] The latter option is no less heinous than the former.[114]

The question is to what extent Mr Blair knew of and was complicit in this

109 Marguerite Feitlowitz, 'The shadow world of a "dirty war"', *Herald International Tribune*, 19-20 August, 2006.

110 Sands, *Lawless World*, supra n 13, pp 205-223.

111 Andreas Whittam Smith, 'Torture Starts at the Top', *The Independent*, 27 February 2006; David Charter, Ruth Gledhill and Greg Hurst, 'Blair condones Amin-Style Tactics Against Terrorism Says Archbishop', *London Times*, 24 February, 2006.

112 Ibid.

113 *Washington Post*, 26 December, 2002.

114 George W Bush acknowledged the existence of a secret CIA prison network (commonly called 'black holes') outside the United States in September 2006; see *The Guardian*, 7 September, 2006.

practice. Having regard to the close co-operation between Mr Bush and Mr Blair, it would be odd if he did not know that the CIA was operating a network of secret 'black sites' and that the suspected terrorists were being sent to those locations. He would know that the sites were located in countries that practised torture. Indeed, it has been pointed out that one of the sites where inmates are subject to violent and coercive interrogation, including beatings, withholding of pain medication, sleep deprivation and loud noise intended to be disorientating, is the British owned island of Diego Garcia in the Indian Ocean.[115]

Furthermore, air logs have confirmed that private jets registered by CIA front companies have landed in England as well as other European countries. In June of 2006, Mr Blair claimed that Parliament had been kept informed of the requests made by the CIA for the transfer of detainees; namely, four in 1998 of which two were granted and two were declined.[116] The reality which he conceded was that he and his Government did not know whether British territory or air space had been used for rendition at any time since 1998. Surprisingly, no systematic record has been kept and the legality of providing assistance to the CIA was not questioned for seven years.[117] But the fact that the full scale of Mr Blair's complacency towards the practice of extraordinary rendition is as yet unearthed does not detract from his known indifference to date.

The second related aspect is the Prime Minister's willingness to deport detainees to countries where torture is known to occur, or even routine, and where there is a real risk that those who are deported will be tortured.

In an effort to avert criticism that these detainees would be in jeopardy of being tortured, Mr Blair announced that the Government would sign agreements with Algeria, Egypt, Jordan and Libya to ensure that Muslim extremists could be returned to their home countries without their dignity or safety being imperilled. 'Should legal obstacles arise,' he said, the Government 'would legislate further including, if necessary, amending the Human Rights Act in respect of the interpretation of the European Convention on Human Rights'.[118]

---

115 Ronald Dworkin, 'Terror and the Attack on Civil Liberties', *The New York Review of Books*, Vol. 50, No. 17, 6 November, 2003.

116 David Rennie, 'Air traffic logs show secret night flights from Kabul and Baghdad, says report', *Daily Telegraph*, 8 June 2006.

117 Martin Bright, 'Rendition: The Cover-up', *New Statesman*, 23 January, 2006, 12. See the memorandum referred to by Bright signed by a private secretary at the Foreign Office addressed to an assistant private secretary at Downing Street confirming that extraordinary rendition is not and never could be legal; disclosing that the papers unearthed 'so far' suggest that 'there could be more such cases'; and affirming that the Foreign Office cannot say that they have received no requests for the use of United Kingdom territory or air space for 'extraordinary rendition'. The memorandum recommends that the attempt be made to shift the focus of people from the 'specifics of rendition' to Condoleezza Rice's clear assurance that United States' activities did not include the use of torture. See also Richard Norton-Taylor, 'Leaked memo reveals strategy to deny knowledge of detention centres', *The Guardian*, 19 January, 2006.

118 *Daily Telegraph*, 6 August, 2005. This comment illustrates Mr Blair's disregard of the rule of law. Dictating an interpretation, or telling the courts how to interpret a document, is constitutionally unsound. Certainly, Parliament may amend the law, and it may do so to effectively reverse a decision of the courts. But it is quite a different matter to dictate to the courts how a document is to be interpreted. That is to usurp the constitutional function of the courts.

Mr Blair has already reneged on his promise to secure agreements with countries believed to practise torture. A number of countries are unwilling to sign such agreements because of the implicit admission that this is their practice. Mr Blair has now, therefore, condoned the deportation of detainees to countries where the Government is satisfied that they will not be subject to torture. The policy is self-evidently disingenuous in that it requires the Government to accept the word of regimes that practise torture but are unwilling to acknowledge that practice. It is impossible to avoid the conclusion that Mr Blair is indifferent to the real possibility that some of the detainees will be in fact tortured.

It would be possible to list as further evidence of Mr Blair's forgiving attitude to torture his amenability to accepting that evidence obtained through torture should be admissible. But for the intervention of the courts,[119] such evidence would have been admissible before the Special Immigration Appeals Commission in assessing the legality of the detention of non-United Kingdom nationals. While, however, Mr Blair may be reasonably comfortable with the distinction between practising torture in Great Britain and admitting evidence obtained through torture practised in another country, at least where the British authorities are unaware of the torture, it is not clear that he was primarily responsible for the legislation in question. The two grounds covered above will suffice; the Prime Minister's complacency, virtually amounting to complicity, towards the United States practice of extraordinary rendition and his willingness to deport detainees suspected of terrorism to countries where there is a real risk that they will be tortured.

Because torture if such a horrendous evil, Mr Blair's indifference, seemingly amounting to a forgiving tolerance of the practice, cannot escape the strongest censure.

(6) Condoning a grotesque post-war economic strategy.

The military and political strategy following the invasion is widely known.[120] I do not intend to focus on the failings of that strategy. Not so widely known is the Bush administration's plans for the economy of a post-war Iraq.

Almost overnight, the Bush administration set out to establish a *laissez-faire* capitalistic Utopia. Neo-conservative economic creed dictated an eviscerated state, a passive workforce, low taxes, no tariffs, open borders and no ownership restrictions. Multi-national corporations would be free to pursue their quest for profit with little or no constraint. What would follow, the reactionary diehards in the White House forecast, would be an economic boom the like of which the World has never seen.

Naomi Klein, in a valuable contribution in *No War: America's Real Business in*

119 *A and others* v. *Secretary of State for the Home Department (No 2)* [2005] UKHL 71. For another instance where the House of Lords firmly upheld a basic human right, i.e. the right not to be discriminated against, see *A (FC) and others (X) FC and Another* v. *Secretary of State for the Home Department ('Belmarsh')* [2004] UKHL 56.

120 Ricks provides a chilling account of the lack of planning and intellectual failure of those behind the invasion of Iraq. See Ricks, *Fiasco*, supra n 1. See also Bob Woodward, *State of Denial*, supra n 1.

Iraq[121] provides details of how Paul Bremer carried out the White House's vision; he immediately fired 500,000 state workers; opened the country's borders to unrestricted imports; and decreed no tariffs, no duties, no inspections and minimal taxes. Numerous state-owned corporations would be privatized on a scale second only to that which followed the collapse of the Soviet Union. Order 37 reduced Iraq's corporate tax rate from approximately 40 per cent to a flat 15 per cent. Order 39 permitted foreign corporations to own 100 per cent of Iraq's assets not in the resource sector and to take 100 per cent of the profits out of the country without being taxed or required to re-invest in the country. Order 40 made the same favourable provision for foreign banks. As Klein wryly observes, all that remained of Saddam Hussein's economic policies was a law restricting trade unions and collective bargaining.

David Ricks refers specifically to Order 2, Dissolution of Iraqi Entities, which formally disbanded several groups: the Iraqi armed forces, which accounted for 385,000 people; the staff of the Ministry of the Interior, which amounted to 285,000 people and included police and domestic security forces; and the presidential security units, a force of some 50,000.[122] Abruptly terminating the livelihood of these people, many of whom were armed, created a vast pool of humiliated, antagonised and politicised men. Bremer's radical privatization programme beginning with the closing of unprofitable state-run industries had the effect of further alienating the middle class, many of whom were managers from those industries.[123]

At the same time, the Bush administration organized lavishly funded seminars throughout the United States promoting the business opportunities pending in the liberated Iraq. Executives from multi-national corporations, such as Halliburton, gave elaborate presentations as to how American companies could compete for multimillion-dollar subcontracts. The free market, it was proclaimed, would drive democracy in Iraq. High ranking military personnel were co-opted to provide optimistically glowing pictures of security in that country.[124] But the administrations expectations were not realized. Whatever their political inclinations in private, hard-nosed businessmen are not prone to indulge in neo-conservative chimeras in the management of their businesses.

The promised economic utopia was never anything other than neo-conservative madness. Out of touch with reality, it was doomed to fail.[125] Indeed, it takes no more than a moment's reflection to predict what would have happened if this economic Utopia had eventuated. Simultaneously the fabric and culture of Iraqi society would have been destroyed. The disharmony between a century's old

---

121 (Gibson Square, 2005), 'Baghdad Year Zero', p 5.

122 Ricks, *Fiasco*, supra n 1, at p 162.

123 Ibid, at pp 165 and 180.

124 Bryan Mealer, 'Dying for Dollars' in *No War: America's Real Business in Iraq*, supra n 121, p 41.

125 This economic strategy was, of course, part of the plan to simply remove Saddam Hussein, establish democracy, and depart the country, a plan which a *New York Times* writer, initially a strong supporter of the war, has written seemed in retrospect to be like a 'childish fantasy', referred to in Hicks, *Fiasco*, supra n 1, at p 380.

civilization and a rabid Chicago-style western economic model would have become rapidly apparent. Eventually, the Iraqi people would have resented the exploitation of their people and resources by corporate America. It may have taken more time to emerge, but this foreign economic occupation would have become as intolerable to them as the present military regime. Insurgency, strife and instability would have been inevitable.

What, then, was Tony Blair's role in this strategy? I am satisfied that he must have known of this economic absurdity and either condoned it or, at the very least, failed to expose and positively reject it. First, it is clear that Mr Bush and Mr Blair were in close contact on all aspects of the proposed war in Iraq. Mr Blair, himself, insisted that the invasion had been subject to 'the most careful planning and consideration'. He claimed that the essential strategic picture was 'unfolding exactly according to plan'.[126] There were also numerous trans-Atlantic discussions between senior officials. It is impossible to accept that the Bush administration's economic strategy was not discussed. Secondly, Mr Blair had to know of the various orders promulgated by Paul Bremer. At no stage is there any record that he evinced any surprise or opposition to these developments.

I have included Mr Blair's knowledge and apparent condoning of the Bush administration's economic strategy for post-war Iraq because it can only be seen as an outright betrayal of the basic tenets of the British Labour Party. It cannot be tenably thought that the Labour Party would have been prepared to condone an economic regime for Iraq which it would reject as utterly inequitable and unacceptable in Great Britain. The inevitable exploitation of the Iraqi people and the country's resources, and the resulting enlargement of the profits of corporate America, would undoubtedly have been anathema to most of its members.

Tony Blair's culpability, therefore, was not just that he condoned an inept economic policy, but that, in supporting the invasion of Iraq, he endorsed a far right economic strategy which effectively betrayed the traditional principles and conscience of the Party he was leading in Government. Moreover, it was an economic strategy which, it is safe to say, would not have had much, if any, greater appeal to the British people as a whole.

The erosion of human rights

de Tocqueville said:

> The idea of rights is nothing but the concept of virtue applied to the world of politics. By means of the idea of rights men have defined the nature of licence and of tyranny … no man can be great without virtue, nor any nation great without respect for rights.[127]

126 Tony Blair, press conference, 26 March, 2003. The two leaders discussed, *inter alia*, the possibility of post-war sectarian violence. Mr Blair accepted Mr Bush's assurance that it was 'unlikely that there would be internecine warfare between the different religious and ethnic groups'. See memorandum written by David Manning summarising the meeting between George W Bush and Tony Blair on 31 January, 2003, reported in the *New York Times*, 17 March, 2006. See also Sands, *Lawless World*, supra n 13, p 281.

127 Alexis de Tocqueville, *Democracy in America* (1835). For a recent translation see Arthur Goldhammer, New York: *Library of America* (Penguin Putman, 2004).

This quotation from de Tocqueville reflects my belief that human rights are paramount and timeless, being grounded in the dignity and worth of the human person. They are an indispensable component of liberal democratic politics, and those politics, even in times of crisis, must recognise individual rights.

The erosion of human rights and civil liberties that has occurred, or which is still threatened by the Blair Government, reflects the same unrealistic and simplistic thinking that motivated Mr Blair to support the war against Iraq.

Focusing on the malevolent role of radical Islamic ideology, the Government strategy was to stress the need for harsh anti-terrorist measures. Civil rights, it was said, must be redrawn as a defence against further terrorist attacks. Mr Blair has been adamant; the balance between national security and individual freedoms must be re-cast in favour of the former. Terrorism poses a crisis and in a crisis the traditional safeguards to individual freedoms must give way to more flexible arrangements. 'The rules of the game', he continues to assert, 'are changing'.[128] As he explained:

> '... when you are in a situation like that [facing the threat of terrorism] you have got to put aside the normal bureaucracy and thinking. If you are constrained by that, forget it, you will never get on top of it at all and you have got to be prepared to knock the rules out of the way in order to get things done'.[129]

It is difficult to imagine a more forthright espousal of expediency over principle, particularly if, for the phrase 'bureaucracy and thinking', one reads the traditional liberties that Great Britain has enjoyed for over eight hundred years.

But Mr Blair's response has proved popular with the public. Whether it is in the domestic context of maintaining law and order or in the context of seeking to combat the threat of terrorism, people in a democracy tend to opt for the generality of harsher laws. The simplistic slogan, 'get tough on crime', is writ large in the cry, 'get tough on terrorism'. The enduring values which the law, and the judiciary, seek to protect are necessarily placed in jeopardy. The greater the threat, or the fear generated by the threat, the greater that jeopardy.

There can be no doubt that human rights would not be imperilled to the extent that they are today if the war in Iraq had never been undertaken. The intensity of the challenge to the rule of law as traditionally understood, to the preservation of fundamental human rights, and to the role and integrity of the judiciary is directly related to that war. Consequently, Mr Blair's culpability in respect of the war has a direct bearing on the erosion of basic liberties which has taken place and which is yet threatened. It is a nasty irony that the threat of terrorist activity, to which the Blair Government's anti-terrorist laws are a reaction, has been seriously exacerbated by the very war Mr Blair claims was necessary to combat terrorism.

While the introduction of firmer measures may be necessary, that necessity

---

128 Tony Blair, press conference, 5 August, 2005. See also Human Rights Watch, 'A new ambivalence toward torture'; 'The rules of the game have changed', *The Guardian*, Editorial, 15 August 2006; and Simon Jenkins, 'The weekend's horror-fest will do Osama bin Ladin's work for him', *The Guardian*, 8 September, 2006.

129 Evidence by Tony Blair to the House of Commons Liaison Committee, 16 July, 2002.

should be clearly demonstrated. The notion that it is the Government's job to give the police the powers they seek to do their job is dangerous unless it is qualified by a close examination of the necessity for the police to have those powers. Civil liberties already eroded, such as the right not to be detained without charge, the exclusion of *habeas corpus*, the deportation of suspects, even when they have been acquitted by an English jury, are serious inroads into fundamental human rights. Executive powers to impose house arrest and other forms of 'control' without charge or trial contravene those rights. Any concession to involve the courts in the implementation of these far-reaching powers simply impairs the independence and integrity of the judiciary.

The key developments which emerge from the Blair Government's anti-terrorist measures can be readily identified. The strategy has had a dramatic impact on the democratic polity.

First, the demand for security is asserted ahead of and at the expense of human rights. The threat of terrorism engenders an apocalyptic vision that is singularly unyielding. As Ronald Dworkin has pointed out, the United States has pursued a strategy of putting safety *absolutely* first.[130] But this is also true of the United Kingdom. Any measure which is seen to improve security against terrorism, even marginally or speculatively, is adopted without apparent or sufficient concern for the harm or unfairness to the victim or its impact on the universal regime of human rights. In a practical sense, the demand for absolute security tends to distort a proper balance being drawn between security and human rights.

Moreover, it is to be noted that the security is, in essence, the security of the majority. No one who is not a Muslim, or not associated with Muslims, is at great risk of being arrested and held as a suspect or deported to their county of origin – or that is the way it is seen. All too easily, the balance can be drawn between the security of the majority and the rights of a minority.[131] Yet, it is a constitutional truism that if you take the protection of the law away from any minority, however different or unpopular, you endanger all minorities and all individuals.

What is needed, and what has been noticeably lacking in Tony Blair's thinking, is an appreciation that, in a democracy, security and human rights are not antithetical values. Security measures can only be justified by the very moral principles that legitimise the state in the first place; the imperative to preserve and protect the liberal democratic constitution. What was required from the Prime Minister was not a cringing supplication to the President of the United States and his administration but the application of the classical theory of human rights that, having due regard to the seriousness of the threat, seeks to find a just balance between order and human rights.

A conception of global justice, which recognises that the powerful possess the ability to determine the fate of the weak, was also required. That justice will not be achieved without allegiance to international law. Yet, faced with the outspoken determination of the Bush administration to challenge global rules, Mr Blair was often silent, and in certain respects, a 'willing handmaiden to some undeniable

130 Dworkin, supra n 115, p 3.
131 Ibid, p 2.

violations of international law'.[132]

The second development has been the assertion of executive power to the detriment of Parliament. Neither Cabinet nor Parliament was effectively involved in the process of formulating the Iraq policy. Nor were they aware of underlying developments, at least, not until after the event. The decisions were the decisions of a small cabal surrounding Mr Blair at No. 10 Downing Street.[133] Put succinctly, they stretched the boundaries of executive power beyond its democratic limits and the bounds of constitutional tolerance.

This assertion of executive power also has the potential to damage the courts. Direct attacks on the judiciary to the effect that 'they just don't get it' necessarily harm the judiciary.[134] Similarly, assertions along the lines that 'the rules of the game are changing',[135] that the 'normal bureaucracy and thinking' and the rules that go with it must be knocked out of the way,[136] and characterizing the judiciary's reaction as 'legal obstacles'[137] necessarily infer that the judiciary is out of touch and failing the community. The essential constitutional balance between the different arms of government is impaired.

Most importantly, this assertion of executive power and the consequential erosion of human rights weakens the democratic process and undermines the very values on which a democracy is founded. It not only diminishes those values but also can bring them into disrepute. There is a real risk that, once individual freedoms are set aside, they will never be regained, and this risk is exacerbated by the apparently endless nature of the war on terror.[138] Nor is respect for fundamental human rights promoted elsewhere in the world when those rights are flouted by a leading democracy. The British Prime Minister's approach provides pabulum to others who wish to break free from the rules.[139]

The third development is related to the effect of this expansion of executive power on the rule of law. It has been observed that at the heart of the Bush administration's policies in Iraq lies the drive for concentrated executive power above the rule of law.[140] Although probably less in intensity, the same drive can be detected in the Blair Government's response to terrorism. The rule of law is being redefined, not by the judiciary, but by the executive. Loss of respect for *habeas corpus* and the rights of suspects and detainees runs counter to the basic ideal of the dignity and worth of the individual person which is the bedrock of the rule of law. Notions of justice are now expected to be sufficiently resilient to

132 Sands, *Lawless World*, supra n 13, pp xii and xviii. Richard A. Clarke, in his book, *Against All Enemies: Inside America's War on Terror* (Free Press, 2004), quotes Bush yelling his head off in a conference; 'I don't care what the international lawyers say, we are going to kick some ass'. (at p 24).

133 Meyer confirms that Tony Blair and his staff dominated the political and military strategy for Iraq; *DC Confidential*, supra n 5, p 239.

134 John Reid reported in *The Guardian*, 10 August, 2006.

135 See above, n 128.

136 See above, n 129.

137 See above, n 118.

138 Kettell, *Dirty Politics*, supra n 2, p 173-174.

139 Sands, *Lawless World*, supra n 13, p 278.

140 Blumenthal, *How Bush Rules*, supra n 1, p 240.

accommodate the executive's demands for secrecy and immunity from judicial supervision. Mr Blair's oft repeated mantra that the 'rules of the game must change'[141] must be understood to mean that it is the rule of law that must change.

All persons sensitive to the need to maintain the rule of law in a working democracy, promote international law, and protect fundamental human rights cannot be other than dismayed at the role and responsibility of Mr Blair in eroding and degrading those concepts.

The 'Indictment'

What, then, are the principle matters to emerge from this survey for which it could be reasonably expected Tony Blair should be accountable. The following list is not a legal indictment, as such; it makes no rigid distinction between political morality, legality or, even, political misjudgement.

1. In supporting the war in Iraq, the Prime Minister allied the United Kingdom, and the Labour Government and Labour Party, with the neo-conservative and ideologically driven administration in the United States. It was beholden on him to assert greater independence and recognize that the policies of the Bush administration were both unrealistic and simplistic.

2. In particular, he effectively endorsed the Bush administration's ill-conceived war model as an appropriate response to the threat of terrorism.

3. The Prime Minister unilaterally committed the United Kingdom to support the United States invasion of Iraq without obtaining the timely sanction of his Cabinet or Parliament. Such sanction as was later obtained was obtained through manipulation and political deceit.

4. In particular, he manipulated the intelligence of the security agencies and was deliberately deceptive when he initially shifted from the claim that Iraq had the potential to develop weapons of mass destruction to the claim that Iraq actually possessed those weapons. Further, his uncritical acceptance of the faith-based intelligence of the Bush administration was inexcusable.

5. In respect of the dossier of September 2002, the Prime Minister deliberately misrepresented the intelligence by omitting the reservations, qualifications and caveats in that intelligence.

6. In particular, his claim that Iraq could launch missiles carrying weapons of mass destruction within 45 minutes was a serious misrepresentation which the Prime Minister must have known was false, or which he came to know was false before he ceased making that claim.

7. The Prime Minister misrepresented, and must have known that he was misrepresenting, the advice which he received from the Attorney-General as to the legality of the war against Iraq. It is impossible to accept that the Prime Minister did not know that there was no sound legal basis for the war. Hence it is difficult to escape the conclusion that he was guilty of the crime of aggression.

8. The Prime Minister has been less than emphatic and, indeed, benignly

141 See above, n 128.

forgiving, in his rejection of the use of torture, principally because of his knowledge of, and effective complicity in, the United States' practice of extraordinary renditions and his insistence on deporting non-nationals to countries where there is a real risk they will be tortured.

9. The Prime Minister, at the very least, condoned the ideological aim of the Bush administration to establish a *laissez-faire* economy which was self-evidently unreal, would have resulted in the exploitation of Iraq's people and resources by corporate America, and would eventually have led to civil instability.

10. The Prime Minister must accept responsibility for the passage of legislation which constitutes an erosion of fundamental human rights unprecedented in recent British history.

11. The Prime Minister has impaired the democratic process in manipulating Cabinet and Parliament, and he must accept responsibility for the unprecedented level of 'spin' used in promoting the war against Iraq. The spin was nothing short of propaganda.

12. In the course of preparing for and supporting the war in Iraq, the Prime Minister displayed an unacceptable disdain for the democratic process, the rule of law and fundamental human rights and civil liberties. The rules of international law have fared no better.

The failure of the political process

The shortcomings in the political process are self-evident in that the Prime Minister was not constrained from committing the above political, immoral and illegal misdemeanours. Nor has he been held accountable for them.

It could be said that Mr Blair has eventually been held accountable in that he is being forced by his own Party, obviously against his will, to relinquish the leadership of the Government earlier than he would himself want. The reason for the pressure on him to resign is because he is now seen as an electoral liability. But, of course, he is seen as a liability largely, although not solely, because of his involvement in the war against Iraq. In this sense, therefore, it could be said his misdeeds have caught up with him. Mr Blair's present troubles in the Labour Party, however, do not absolve the political system from the charge that it failed.

Primary political responsibility in a democracy rests with the electorate, and it is true that, although his credibility was seriously in issue, Tony Blair was returned for a third term in the General Election in 2005. While the war in Iraq was a critical issue for a large and growing number of voters, the Prime Minister's conduct leading up to the war did not dominate the campaigning. Both the Labour and Conservative parties were reluctant to raise the subject because of their earlier pro-war stance, and the Liberal Democrats, who did take up the issue, were anxious not to be characterized as a one issue party. The election was far from a plebiscite on the war. A number of domestic issues of likely greater concern to many people were hotly debated.[142] In the result, Tony Blair was re-elected on a

---

142 See Kettell, *Dirty Politics*, supra n 2, pp 164-165.

significantly low voter turn out and with a substantially reduced majority. As W. G. Runciman has observed, it no longer made much difference to the majority of the electorate whether the Labour Party or the Conservative Party was in power.[143]

The essential point, however, is that the verdict of the electorate is circumscribed by the extent to which it is informed. People are not immune to manipulation and being deceived by a prime minister or a government bent on manipulation and deception. The question therefore remains open; would the electorate have returned Tony Blair at all if more people had been aware of the culpability on his part as demonstrated above.

A further factor reducing the impact of the ultimate electoral sanction which the electorate can impose is the seemingly inevitable time lag that occurs before some matters seep into the public's consciousness. The old political adage: 'You can fool some of the people all of the time, and all of the people some of the time, but you cannot fool all of the people all of the time',[144] reflects this time lag. This perception, of course, is evident in the tardy desire within the Labour Party for Tony Blair to vacate the leadership and in the belated decline in support for Republican Congressman and Senators in the recent mid-term elections in the United States. It is axiomatic that this delay in public reaction will be reduced if the public is better informed earlier in time. That objective can only be achieved if the political system is transparent and has the capacity to scrutinise and publicise any real or apparent prime ministerial, ministerial or executive maladministration or mendaciousness, if not contemporaneously, as soon thereafter as is possible.

Having regard to the Prime minister's culpability, Mr Blair, in a properly functioning democracy, would have been called upon to resign the premiership in Parliament. When one considers the peccadilloes and administrative mishaps which have caused Ministers to step down in the past, it is incongruous that Mr Blair has not resigned, or been forced to resign, for a war which was based on a delusion, and which has had such calamitous and humanly tragic consequences. In short, he has not been held accountable in Parliament for the manipulation of the intelligence or for the deception which he practised in pursuit of the war.

At once it must be acknowledged that, if the occupation and post-war rehabilitation of Iraq had been successful, it would be unrealistic to expect the Prime Minister to have been held to account. In the wake of a united and stable Iraq holding the beacon for democracy and freedom in the Middle East, Mr Blair's mendaciousness would have been overlooked, minimized or forgiven. As disturbing as it is to admit, the end would be seen to have justified the means.

But far from being a success, the war has been an unmitigated and tragic disaster. His policies having failed, the Prime Minister cannot now escape responsibility for his pre-war misconduct. The end proved an illusion and Mr Blair should have been held accountable for the undemocratic and unacceptable means that he adopted in pursuit of that illusion. The fact that he was neither monitored

143 W. G. Runciman, 'What happened to the Labour Party?' *London Review of Books*, 22 June 2006, pp 17 and 19.

144 Attributed to Abraham Lincoln, 16th President of the United States (1809-1865).

nor curbed at the time, nor subsequently held accountable, is the measure of the failure of the parliamentary process.

The deaths, human suffering and dislocation have proved a calamity. One shies away from citing figures of the servicemen and women killed or injured or the civilians killed or injured in Iraq simply because, by the time this essay is read, those figures will be out of date. Furthermore, uncertainty exists as to the number of civilian deaths because of the allies' shameful neglect to put in place a policy or system to collect the appropriate data.[145] Suffice it to say, that hundreds of troops have died or been wounded[146] and thousands of civilians, including children, have been killed or wounded.[147] Over a million Iraqi people have fled Iraq, that is, more than 1,000 a day, and over another million been displaced internally.[148] Millions live in daily fear and trepidation for themselves and their families. Millions, including the young and impressionable, are scarred by hate, hostility and an immunity to, and even an insatiable appetite for, violence. And still the carnage and social disruption continues. The exact figures do not matter; the cost has been too great to justify the regime change that has taken place.

Apart from the human cost, the war has galvanized Islamic extremism; destroyed the infrastructure and basic services of the country; provided a fertile breeding and recruiting ground for terrorists; exacerbated the religious divisions in the country; created extreme instability fomenting a civil war; inflamed hatred of the West; rendered Iraq receptive to Iranian fundamentalist influence; resulted in a higher level of torture than in the days of Saddam Hussein; placed the armed forces in a no-win situation without any real prospect of emerging from Iraq with a semblance of military honour; provided a diversion from what should have been the primary task of dealing with the real threat, Al Qaeda; diverted a massive amount of money which could have been more profitably expended in more directly confronting that organisation and threatened terrorist activity;[149] weakened

145 For reported civilian deaths on ongoing basis, see the Iraq Body Count Database, www.iraqbodycount.org/database/

146 As at the beginning of 2007, 3000 members of the United State's military have died since the beginning of the Iraq war in March 2003. Over the same period the British military has reported 126 deaths. See also, 'U S military deaths in Iraq hit 2,875', *The Associated Press*, 27 November, 2006.

147 Estimates of civilian deaths vary from 100,000 to 655,000. See, e.g. David Brown, 'Study claims Iraq's "excess" death toll has reached 655,000', *Washington Post*, 11 October, 2006. See also, 'The Lancet surveys of mortality before and after the 2003 invasion of Iraq', http/en.wikipedia.org/wiki/lancet_surveys_of_mortality_before_and_after_the_2003_invasion_of_Iraq. A recent report claims that over 100 Iraqis are being killed everyday. See Patrick Cockburn, '100 Iraqis being killed each day, says UN', *The Independent*, 26 July, 2006.

148 The United Nations Commissioner for Refugees has reported that 1.8 million people have fled Iraq to neighbouring countries and 1.6 million people have been displaced internally. See *ABC News On Line*, 4 November, 2006, See also Walter Pincus, '1,000 Iraqis a Day Flee Violence. U. N. Group Finds', *Washington Post*, 24 November, 2006

149 Ricks relates that during 2004 and 2005 the cost of the Iraq war to the American taxpayer was running at about $5 billion a month meaning that, by mid-2006, the total cost of the venture had surpassed $200 billion. He states that it is staggering to think how that amount of money could have been spent differently to achieve the stated goals of countering terrorism and curtailing the proliferation of weapons of mass destruction. He suggests, by way of an example, that just $1 billion in aid might have changed the face of education in Pakistan and helped draw out the poison of anti-Western teachings in that country. Ricks, *Fiasco*, supra n 1, at p 431.

the capacity of the United States and the West to respond to the state-based threats to the peace and security of the world as, for example, in Iran and North Korea; diverted and sapped resources required to meet the resurgence of the Taliban in Afghanistan; damaged the relationship of America's allies with the United States and potentially damaged the relationship of the United Kingdom with the United States; provided sustenance elsewhere in the world for those who would deny human rights; and, in all, made the world a less safe place for decades to come if not the remainder of this century.

The verdict of history will undoubtedly be harsh, but what was required was a verdict within the political process that would maintain the effectiveness and integrity of the democratic system. It is that verdict which has not been forthcoming.

The reasons why Mr Blair was not subject to a compelling demand for his resignation are disturbing. One possibility is that Parliament did not fully appreciate the extent of the Prime Minister's manipulation and deception. But, if that was so, it was because the manipulation and deception was successful. Parliament, it must be accepted, can be deceived, and the machinery is not in place to expose the deception, particularly if the Prime Minister's own Party, or the majority of them, remain resolutely loyal. Another possibility is that the question of the Prime Minister's culpability was unnecessarily confused with the pros and cons of invading Iraq. Initial support for the war may have inhibited the Opposition and many Members of Parliament from questioning the means by which Mr Blair pursued and prosecuted the war. Demanding Mr Blair's resignation could all too easily be seen as an admission that they were wrong. Either way, the prognosis for the health of democracy is bleak.

The failure to hold Mr Blair to account has also pointed up a wider systemic failure. Not only has no other Minister resigned, but no official has been held responsible for any of the controversies surrounding the conflict in Iraq. Indeed, some officials who shared in the decisions have been promoted.[150] If one can imagine a domestic event involving a similar catastrophe brought about by a similar level of manipulation and deception, it is certain that heads would roll. Of course, if Mr Blair, as the main perpetrator, remains untouched it is impossible, or at least extremely difficult, to bring those who played a lesser role to account.

In the face of a Prime Minister exerting a monolithic control over foreign policy, including a resolute measure of secrecy, Parliament lacked the machinery to effectively monitor his actions or hold him to account. While parliamentary questions can be a useful tool to control or curb the excesses of executive power, the effectiveness of this mechanism is restricted by the constraints of time and the executive's control over official information, not to mention Ministers' ability to evade direct answers. Similarly, the effectiveness of parliamentary committees is limited by their composition in accordance with the parties' strength in the House of Commons, by their inability to scrutinize Ministers or senior public servants without government

150 E.g. John Scarlett, who was head of the JIC at the time the first dossier was prepared, was appointed head of the British Secret Intelligence Service (MI6) on 6 May, 2004.

permission and by their lack of power to compel the disclosure of information the government may choose to call 'sensitive'.[151] Nor, while select committees may issue reports, can they ensure that the report will be debated in Parliament.

The shortcomings of the select committee process to properly determine a question such as the one the Foreign Affairs Committee set for itself immediately following the publication of the claims of the then BBC journalist, Andrew Gilligan,[152] are readily apparent. The question was valid; that is, whether the Government had 'presented accurate and complete information to Parliament in the period leading up to military action in Iraq, particularly in respect of weapons of mass destruction'.[153] But the Committee was frustrated at every turn. Its requests to interview John Scarlett and Richard Dearlove were refused. Tony Blair declined to be interviewed. He also initially refused to allow Alastair Campbell to be interviewed.[154] Requests to see draft copies of the first dossier and intelligence material were rejected. National security considerations were put forward to justify these refusals, although it is difficult to see how the earlier drafts of the dossier, at least in large part, could attract this excuse. In the result, the Foreign Secretary appeared before the Committee and outlined 'some extracts' of what was considered to be the 'relevant' sections of the intelligence assessments of the JIC.[155]

Nor, as at the time of writing, has a commission of inquiry been appointed and empowered to inquire into the Prime Minister's decision to support the invasion of Iraq and the legality of the war. Independent commissions of inquiry can serve a valuable democratic function in investigating and determining facts, uncovering maladministration and the abuse of power, exposing dishonest or fraudulent malpractice and, generally, educating the public.[156] Neither the Hutton nor Butler Inquiries served this function in respect of the political issues behind the decisions to invade Iraq.[157] Nor have the legality of the war and the saga of the Attorney-General's twofold advice been independently examined. The terms of reference in both inquiries were deliberately drawn narrowly so as to preclude any examination of these wider, but critical, issues. Lord Hutton and Lord Butler adhered to the letter of their respective remits.[158] In the result, the more far-

151 Kettell, *Dirty Politics*, supra n 2, p 17.

152 Andrew Gilligan, 6:07 broadcast for *Today*, BBC Radio 4, 29 May, 2003.

153 *The Decision to go to War in Iraq*, Foreign Affairs Committee, Ninth Report of Session 2002-2003, 7 July 2003, paras. 1-7.

154 Subsequently, Mr Campbell was permitted to appear. See Kettell, *Dirty Politics*, supra n 2, p 122.

155 Foreign Affairs Committee Report, supra n 153, para. 6.

156 The value of commissions of inquiry inquiring into governmental activity is seriously reduced by the absence of any mechanism for the independent appointment of the chairperson and members. There can be little doubt that the power to appoint the membership of a commission of inquiry, especially the chairperson, can be a significant, if not decisive, factor in determining the outcome of an inquiry. The ability to frame the terms of reference can have an equally disabling or disarming impact.

157 Kettell, *Dirty Politics*, supra n 2, p 7.

158 Lord Hutton expressly approbated the narrowly drawn focus of his inquiry on the basis that, for the purposes of practicality 'you have to draw the line somewhere'. He did not permit Mr Blair to be cross-examined. Lord Butler announced that the inquiry would focus on processes and systems rather than on the actions of specific individuals. Kettell, supra, n 2, pp 143-145.

reaching inquiry into what must be acknowledged has been the greatest foreign policy débâcle in recent times has never taken place. In a properly functioning democracy the absence of such an inquiry would be, or certainly should be, unthinkable.

Not unexpectedly, Mr Blair has triumphantly claimed to have been vindicated by the Hutton and Butler Reports. Strangely, his claims suggest that the inquiries had much wider terms of reference than was the case. Even so, a cursory reading of the Reports indicates serious areas of concern. Lord Butler, for example, commented on the 'relative thinness of the intelligence base' and concluded that the first dossier had taken the intelligence to 'the outer limits'. 'More weight,' he added, 'was placed on the intelligence than it could bear'.[159] This is a curiously reticent way of explaining the suppression of the many reservations, qualifications and caveats in the intelligence at the time. He also noted that the JIC chairman should be someone with experience of dealing with Ministers in a very senior role, and 'who is demonstrably beyond influence'.[160] This, again, seems an oddly restrained way of indicating that John Scarlett, the then Chairperson of the JIC, had failed to counter the strengthening of the intelligence 'from a presentational point of view'.[161]

Again, Lord Butler observed that the centralized structure of the Government had the effect of concentrating 'detailed knowledge and effective decision-making in fewer minds at the top.'[162] The 'informality and circumscribed character of the Government's procedures' had risked 'reducing the scope for informed political judgement'.[163] In other, and in more direct words, this misgiving describes the Prime Minister's presidential and élite style of governance in which a small group of select advisers surrounding him at number 10 Downing Street made the critical decisions divorced from any effective input from Cabinet or Parliament. Then, Lord Butler's exculpatory finding that there was 'no evidence of deliberate distortion or of culpable negligence' seems to be oddly against the weight of evidence[164] unless the phrases 'deliberate distortion' and 'culpable negligence' are fixed with illiberal meanings. Certainly, numerous questions went unanswered. Perhaps Lord Butler's scrutiny of the facts was undermined by his adamant refusal from the outset to apportion any blame or responsibility to any specific individual.

It nevertheless remains undeniable that the conduct of the Prime Minister and his immediate advisers had the effect of blurring the boundaries between the political function of governance and the function of the intelligence gathering services. To properly serve its function, the latter must be separate and

159 *Butler Report*, supra n 24, paras. 327, 331 and 464-466.

160 Ibid, paras. 469 and 597.

161 I consider that it was inappropriate for Alastair Campbell to have presided at meetings concerned with intelligence and the preparation of a document purportedly containing intelligence, which would have the imprimatur of the intelligence services. The arrangement underestimates the influence a forceful and competent person can exert when chairing a meeting.

162 *Butler Report*, supra n 24, Section 7.4.

163 Ibid.

164 Ibid, para. 450.

independent of political machinations. Intelligence, to be intelligence, cannot be influenced by politicians who may have, and are likely to have, an extraneous objective. Intelligence which is subject to such influence is contaminated intelligence. Those responsible for that contamination, such as Tony Blair and his close team of advisers in this instance, not only pervert the democratic process, but also undermine the security of the state.

But if the system was inadequate to curb Mr Blair's behaviour and Parliament did not intervene to call him to account, there still remains the Labour Party.

Political parties are an integral part of the political process, and the Labour Party cannot escape censure. Certainly, a group of 121 Labour back-benchers staged something of a rebellion in defying the parties whip and supporting a motion that the case for war was 'as yet unproven',[165] but the move was more a symbol of defiance and frustration than a serious threat to Mr Blair's position. Most within the Party remained supine and must stand condemned as craven for allowing Mr Blair to remain for as long as he has and to then depart on agreed terms, albeit under pressure. Gratitude to Tony Blair for past triumphs, members' self interest, misplaced loyalty, and the desire not to haemorrhage the Party, cannot excuse the Party's inaction. The Party has only itself to blame if many conclude that it has forfeited the moral high ground by not ousting a leader who led it, and the country, into a war which is illegal, immoral and unjust by means which were dishonest. Its inaction has put in jeopardy the credibility and self respect of the Labour Party as a party of principle, justice and humanity.

Nor is it any excuse for the Party to retreat to its Constitution designed to ensure an orderly succession in the leadership. As Mr Blair's lack of probity became more widely known or suspected, members should have recognised that an exceptional response was called for. It will be a shameful footnote to history that there was no-one in the Parliamentary Labour Party who, with sufficient support to command a chorus, did not rise in the House and resoundingly voice the words of Leo Amery to Neville Chamberlain all those years ago: 'You have sat too long here for any good you have been doing. Depart, I say, and let us have done with you. In the name of God, go!'[166]

The finding is inevitable that both Parliament and the Labour Party have failed the democratic imperative. Tony Blair, in foreign policy, exerted unbridled and unchecked power to pursue his personal vision. When that vision was threatened he was able to manipulate the political process to his own ends.

But the end was flawed and the means dishonest, and we have yet to learn the full cost.

---

165 Kettell, *Dirty Politics*, supra n 2, p 96.

166 Leo Amery, Conservative backbencher during the 'Norway Debate' in the House of Commons on 7-8th May, 1940, *Official Report* (Hansard) 5th Series, Vol. 360, columns 1073-1196 and 1251-1366.

Blair's Impeachment

Alex Salmond MP

Alex Salmond is the leader of the Scottish National Party. He joined with MPs from other parties in moves to impeach Prime Minister Blair. Here he outlines the background to those moves.

As Tony Blair freeloaded his way around Europe over the summer of 2004, two noted academics prepared a devastating report* for a cross-party group of MPs. This report not only details the Prime Minister's misdemeanours over Iraq but also points to a parliamentary mechanism that could have finally held him to account over the abuse of his office in launching the war.

This is not the whitewash of a Hutton or the establishment report of a Butler. This is the painstaking, forensic examination of academics – Glen Rangwala and Dan Plesch – who examine the detailed and growing public record and then find the Prime Minister guilty of repeated breaches of his responsibilities of office.

The reports by Lords Hutton and Butler did at least contain evidence which shone new light into the recesses of government decision-making and published a range of intelligence information for the first time.

It is thus now possible to see exactly what the government and this Prime Minister knew about Iraq, and when they knew it.

The report finds that the Prime Minister exaggerated the condition of Iraq's illicit weapons well beyond the assessments of the intelligence services or the United Nations inspectors.

In this case, there is the clearest evidence from information in the public domain that Tony Blair not only misled parliament, but had also entered into a prior agreement with George Bush to go to war in Iraq.

Add to these charges the negligence and incompetence shown throughout this sorry affair, the thousands of coalition soldiers who have died, and the tens of thousands of Iraqi dead.

The case is that the Prime Minister made 28 statements about Iraq's weapons that were not supported by the intelligence assessments available to him. To give but one example, on 17 September 2002, his chief of staff, Jonathan Powell, wrote in an e-mail that when publishing the intelligence dossier the Government needed to make it clear that:

> 'we do not claim that we have evidence that he – Saddam Hussein – is an imminent threat'.

One week later, however, when the Prime Minister presented the dossier to the House of Commons, he said that the threat was 'serious and current'. It is impossible to reconcile the e-mail from the Prime Minister's chief of staff with the statement that the Prime Minister made to the House a week later.

Twelve occasions documented in *A Case to Answer* show that the Prime Minister failed either to disclose available counter-evidence or to ensure that it came into the public domain. I was particularly struck by the case of Saddam Hussein's ill-fated son-in-law, Hussein Kamel, who was often cited by the Prime Minister as providing evidence for the possession of weapons of mass destruction. However, we now know, from the Butler inquiry, that British intelligence had access to information that he gave the UN weapons inspectors on 7 August 1995, when he said that he had personally ordered the destruction of weapons of mass destruction. That information proved to be correct, but the point is that, although available, it was not presented to the House or to the wider public.

Butler expressed great surprise at the failure formally to withdraw material that was found to be false until much later in the process – even now the Prime Minister is disinclined to tell us when that particular fact became available to him. And there's the question of whether the Prime Minister entered into an agreement with the United States without the consent of Cabinet, Parliament or the people.

I was struck by *Plan of Attack,* which was written by Bob Woodward – who was involved in a previous impeachment – with the compliance of the White House, and describes events in September 2002. It states:

> 'On the morning of Sept. 7, 2002 Blair left London on a transatlantic flight to see Bush at Camp David. In Blair's conversations with Bush, it was increasingly clear to the Prime Minister how committed Bush was to action … Bush looked Blair in the eye. "Saddam Hussein is a threat. And we must work together to deal with this threat, and the world will be better off without him." Bush recalled that he was "probing" and "pushing" the Prime Minister. He said it might require – would probably entail – war. Blair might have to send British troops. "I'm with you", the Prime Minister replied, looking Bush back in the eye, pledging flat out to commit British military force if necessary, the critical promise that Bush had been seeking.'

If we believe that account or, even more pertinently, the other information now in the public domain, it is nothing like what the House of Commons was then being told. Any reasonable person would at least conclude from the dossier and the mass of information that there was a process whereby Parliament was not told the truth and that there is a case to answer.

With the imminent departure of the Prime Minister, it would seem he will escape impeachment – whether the Labour Party escapes the judgement of the people during the local, Scottish and Welsh elections is another matter entirely.

**Published as* A Case to Answer *and available from Spokesman (www.spokesmanbooks.com) price £5.*

A Pre-emptive Lie

Adam Price MP

Last October, the Plaid MP Adam Price moved the motion calling for an inquiry into 'the way in which the responsibilities of Government were discharged in relation to Iraq and all matters relevant thereto, in the period leading up to military action in that country in March 2003 and in its aftermath' (see Spokesman 93*). He had earlier helped initiate the campaign to impeach Tony Blair for High Crimes and Misdemeanours in relation to the invasion of Iraq. These excerpts are taken from his address to the People's Assembly, which was organised by the Stop the War Coalition at Westminster Central Hall in March 2007.*

Over the road at the moment in Parliament, in the House of Commons, they're debating the abolition of slavery 200 years ago. This is some kind of metaphor for the reason behind today's event. There they are, discussing rather ponderously an injustice that was put right two hundred years ago, while they're refusing to discuss an injustice that is ongoing every day in Iraq and Afghanistan at the moment.

It's rather odd that Tony Blair feels he can say sorry for the wrongs of past generations, but not utter a single word of apology for his own actions himself. A political apology has a time lag of 200 years in this country.

Blair is leaving the political stage as we speak, and not a moment too soon. But look who's queuing up to move in – Gordon Brown and David Cameron – who backed the war and have themselves refused to apologise to the people of this country and to the people of Iraq. They don't want to talk about it

The decision to go to war, they think, is water under the bridge. But how can it be 'water under the bridge', when every day people are still drowning, when every day our presence there in that country is a violent provocation, when every day their silence – Cameron and Brown's – makes a mockery and a sham of democracy in this country.

But there are politicians prepared to speak up. In Spain, rebel members of the Conservative *Partido Popular* have said for the first time that the war was wrong. Michael Ancram, who voted against Trident, has said that we should talk to Hamas, and has called for the immediate withdrawal of British troops from Iraq. Michael Ancram! I remember Michael Ancram. He was the Shadow Foreign Secretary who summed up for the Opposition that was no Opposition on the night of the fateful decision to support the war in Iraq. What a Damascene conversion – I know he was summing up because I was heckling him at the time – but he now agrees with us. And the Australian Labour Party once again has called for the withdrawal of Australian troops from Iraq.

There is movement even in places like Parliament. We heard at the beginning of the day Dennis Kucinich, the US Congressman and anti-war candidate for the Democratic Party Presidential nomination, telling us that this is a moment of decision, and I know that he is right. The decisions that we make today, the action that we fail to take, will cast a long shadow over the rest of this century, and will if we're not careful come back to hurt us and to haunt us.

Firstly, as we heard, our reliance on nuclear weapons, and the vote on Trident, will spawn twenty or thirty new nuclear states. Because the signal we're sending to other nations is that we will pulverise you unless you develop your own weapons of mass destruction. That is the signal we're sending to every repressive regime on the planet.

Secondly, arms exports: our shameful role as the world's second biggest arms exporter means that we are contributing more than most towards sowing the seeds of conflict in this world, and all with the support of a Labour government that thinks that saving jobs is somehow more important than saving lives.

Thirdly, the war on terror. The first war in history that created the very thing it was meant to defeat. The number of terror attacks is up seven times on what they were before the invasion of Iraq.

And finally, look at our record of backing repressive regimes across the world, because it suits our present purpose. That throws up a reservoir of resentment amongst the young people in those countries. Where is our passion for democracy and human rights when we are shoring up the corrupt regime in Saudi Arabia? We have a delegation in Parliament as we speak from Kazakhstan, again a regime with a terrible record in human rights, but a convenient ally in the so-called war on terror.

So what must change? Instead of exporting arms we should convert our military industry to civilian use. We should stop training the armies of human rights abusers, abolish nuclear weapons and use the savings to invest in international aid. We should reform the UN to allow fair representation for poorer countries, and allow ordinary people's voices to be heard so that people's assemblies right across the planet can be heard. We should stop trying to maintain this cruel imperial fiction that we 'punch above our weight'.

Instead of trying to remain a great power, we should become a power for good.

And finally we should support the efforts to have the crime of aggression written into the statue of the International Criminal Court. Why? Because we know that this terrible war in Iraq wasn't a pre-emptive attack to prevent war, it was a pre-emptive lie to promote war, and the man that was responsible needs to answer for his crime.

The Lancet Survey

Truth will out

Richard Horton

The Lancet *survey of mortality in Iraq caused great controversy when it was first published in 2004 (see* Spokesman 84*). The British Government sought to rubbish its methodology and its findings that about 100,000 civilians had died as a result of the invasion of that country. A further, more extensive study was published in the same journal in October 2006, by which time an estimated 650,000 Iraqi civilians had died. Now, it has become clear the Government was disregarding not only the findings of* The Lancet *studies, but also the advice of its own statisticians that the methodology that was used was 'robust'. The editor of* The Lancet *draws the conclusions.*

Our collective failure has been to take our political leaders at their word. The BBC has now reported that the government's own scientists advised ministers that the Johns Hopkins study on Iraq civilian mortality was accurate and reliable, following a freedom of information request by the reporter Owen Bennett-Jones. This paper was published in the *Lancet* last October. It estimated that 650,000 Iraqi civilians had died since the American and British led invasion in March 2003.

Immediately after publication, the Prime Minister's official spokesman said that the *Lancet's* study 'was not one we believe to be anywhere near accurate'. The Foreign Secretary, Margaret Beckett, said that the *Lancet* figures were 'extrapolated' and a 'leap'. President Bush said: 'I don't consider it a credible report'.

Scientists at the United Kingdom's Department for International Development thought differently. They concluded that the study's methods were 'tried and tested'. Indeed, the Johns Hopkins approach would likely lead to an 'underestimation of mortality'.

The Ministry of Defence's chief scientific adviser said the research was 'robust', close to 'best practice', and 'balanced'. He recommended 'caution in publicly criticising the study'.

When these recommendations went to the Prime Minister's advisers, they were horrified. One person briefing Tony Blair wrote: 'Are we really sure that the report is likely to be right? That is certainly what the brief implies?' A Foreign and Commonwealth Office official was forced to conclude that the government 'should not be rubbishing the *Lancet*'.

The Prime Minister's adviser finally gave in. He wrote: 'The survey methodology used here cannot be rubbished, it is a tried and tested way of measuring mortality in conflict zones'.

How would the Government respond? Would it welcome the Johns Hopkins study as an important contribution to understanding the military threat to Iraqi civilians? Would it ask for urgent independent verification? Would it invite the Iraqi government to upgrade civilian security?

Of course, our Government did none of these things. Tony Blair was advised to say: 'The overriding message is that there are no accurate or reliable figures of deaths in Iraq'.

His official spokesman went further and rejected the Johns Hopkins report entirely. It was a shameful and cowardly dissembling by a Labour – yes, by a Labour – Prime Minister.

Indeed, it was even contrary to the United States' own Iraq Study Group report, which concluded last year that 'there is significant underreporting of the violence in Iraq'.

This Labour Government, which includes Gordon Brown as much as it does Tony Blair, is party to a war crime of monstrous proportions. Yet our political consensus prevents any judicial or civil society response. Britain is paralysed by its own indifference.

At a time when we are celebrating our enlightened abolition of slavery 200 years ago, we are continuing to commit one of the worst international abuses of human rights of the past half-century. It is inexplicable how we allowed this to happen. It is inexplicable why we are not demanding this Government's mass resignation.

Two hundred years from now, the Iraq war will be mourned as the moment when Britain violated its delicate democratic constitution and joined the ranks of nations that use extreme pre-emptive killing as a tactic of foreign policy. Some anniversary that will be.

The article first appeared in The Guardian *on 28 March 2007. It is re-printed here by kind permission of the author.*

Ensuring Obedience

Noam Chomsky interviewed by Michael Shank

Noam Chomsky is Professor of Linguistics at the Massachusetts Institute of Technology. Michael Shank is the policy director for the 3D Security Initiative. His questions are printed in italic type, and Professor Chomsky's replies in ordinary type.

With similar nuclear developments in North Korea and Iran, why has the United States pursued direct diplomacy with North Korea but refuses to do so with Iran?

To say that the United States has pursued diplomacy with North Korea is a little bit misleading. It did under the Clinton administration, though neither side completely lived up to their obligations. Clinton didn't do what was promised, nor did North Korea, but they were making progress. So when Bush came into the presidency, North Korea had enough uranium or plutonium for maybe one or two bombs, but then very limited missile capacity. During the Bush years it's exploded. The reason is, he immediately cancelled the diplomacy and he's pretty much blocked it ever since.

They made a very substantial agreement in September 2005 in which North Korea agreed to eliminate its enrichment programmes and nuclear development completely. In return the United States agreed to terminate the threats of attack and to begin moving towards the planning for the provision of a light water reactor, which had been promised under the framework agreement. But the Bush administration instantly undermined it. Right away, they cancelled the international consortium that was planning for the light water reactor, which was a way of saying we're not going to agree to this agreement. A couple of days later they started attacking the financial transactions of various banks. It was timed in such a way to make it clear that the United States was not going to move towards its commitment to improve relations. And of course it never withdrew the threats. So that was the end of the September 2005 agreement.

That one is now coming back, just in the last few days (February 2007). The way it's portrayed in the US media is, as usual with the government's party line, that North Korea is now perhaps a little more amenable to accept the September 2005 proposal. So there's some optimism. If you go across the Atlantic, to the *Financial Times*, to review the same events they point out that an embattled Bush administration, it's their phrase, needs some kind of victory, so maybe it'll be willing to move towards diplomacy. It's a little more accurate I think if you look at the background.

But there is some minimal sense of optimism about it. If you look back over the record – and North Korea is a horrible place, nobody is arguing about that – on this issue they've been pretty rational. It's been a kind of tit-for-tat history. If the United States is accommodating, the North Koreans become accommodating. If the United States is hostile, they become hostile. That's reviewed pretty well by Leon Sigal, who's one of the leading specialists on this, in a recent issue of *Current History*. But that's been the general picture and we're now at a place where there could be a settlement on North Korea.

That's much less significant for the United States than Iran. The Iranian issue I don't think has much to do with nuclear weapons frankly. Nobody is saying Iran should have nuclear weapons – nor should anybody else. But the point in the Middle East, as distinct from North Korea, is that this is centre of the world's energy resources. Originally the British and secondarily the French had dominated it, but after the Second World War, it's been a US preserve. That's been an axiom of US foreign policy, that it must control Middle East energy resources. It is not a matter of access as people often say. Once the oil is on the seas it goes anywhere. In fact if the United States used no Middle East oil, it'd have the same policies. If we went on solar energy tomorrow, it'd keep the same policies. Just look at the internal record, or the logic of it, the issue has always been control. Control is the source of strategic power.

Dick Cheney declared in Kazakhstan or somewhere that control over pipeline is a 'tool of intimidation and blackmail'. When we have control over the pipelines it's a tool of benevolence. If other countries have control over the sources of energy and the distribution of energy then it is a tool of intimidation and blackmail, exactly as Cheney said. And that's been understood as far back as George Kennan and the early post-war days when he pointed out that if the United States controls Middle East resources, it'll have veto power over its industrial rivals. He was speaking particularly of Japan, but the point generalizes.

So Iran is a different situation. It's part of the major energy system of the world.

So when the United States considers a potential invasion you think it's under the premise of gaining control? That is what the United States will gain from attacking Iran?

There are several issues in the case of Iran. One is simply that it is independent and independence is not tolerated. Sometimes it's called successful defiance in the internal record. Take Cuba. A very large majority of the US population is in favour of establishing diplomatic relations with Cuba and has been for a long time with some fluctuations. And even part of the business world is in favour of it too. But the government won't allow it. It's attributed to the Florida vote but I don't think that's much of an explanation. I think it has to do with a feature of world affairs that is insufficiently appreciated. International affairs is very much run like the mafia. The godfather does not accept disobedience, even from a small storekeeper who doesn't pay his protection money. You have to have obedience otherwise the idea can spread that you don't have to listen to the orders and it can spread to important places.

If you look back at the record, what was the main reason for the US attack on Vietnam? Independent development can be a virus that can infect others. That's the way it's been put, Kissinger in this case, referring to Allende in Chile. And with Cuba it's explicit in the internal record. Arthur Schlesinger, presenting the report of the Latin American Study Group to incoming President Kennedy, wrote that the danger is the spread of the Castro idea of taking matters into your own hands, which has a lot of appeal to others in the same region that suffer from the same problems. Later internal documents charged Cuba with successful defiance of US policies going back 150 years – to the Monroe Doctrine – and that can't be tolerated. So there's kind of a state commitment to ensuring obedience.

Going back to Iran, it's not only that it has substantial resources and that it's part of the world's major energy system, but it also defied the United States. The United States, as we know, overthrew the parliamentary government, installed a brutal tyrant, was helping him develop nuclear power, in fact the very same programmes that are now considered a threat were being sponsored by the US government, by Cheney, Wolfowitz, Kissinger, and others, in the 1970s, as long as the Shah was in power. But then the Iranians overthrew him, and they kept US hostages for several hundred days. And the United States immediately turned to supporting Saddam Hussein and his war against Iran as a way of punishing Iran. The United States is going to continue to punish Iran because of its defiance. So that's a separate factor.

And again, the will of the US population and even US business is considered mostly irrelevant. Seventy five per cent of the population here favours improving relations with Iran, instead of threats. But this is disregarded. We don't have polls from the business world, but it's pretty clear that the energy corporations would be quite happy to be given authorisation to go back into Iran instead of leaving all that to their rivals. But the state won't allow it. And it is setting up confrontations right now, very explicitly. Part of the reason is strategic, geopolitical, economic, but part of the reason is the mafia complex. They have to be punished for disobeying us.

Venezuela has been successfully defiant with Chavez making a swing towards socialism. Where are they on our list?

They're very high. The United States sponsored and supported a military coup to overthrow the government. In fact, that's its last, most recent effort in what used to be a conventional resort to such measures.

But why haven't we turned our sights more towards Venezuela?

They're there. There's a constant stream of abuse and attack by the government and therefore the media, who are almost reflexively against Venezuela. For several reasons. Venezuela is independent. It's diversifying its exports to a limited extent, instead of just being dependent on exports to the United States. And it's initiating moves towards Latin American integration and independence. It's what they call a Bolivarian alternative and the United States doesn't like any of that.

This again is defiance of US policies going back to the Monroe Doctrine. There's now a standard interpretation of this trend in Latin America, another kind of party line. Latin America is all moving to the left, from Venezuela to Argentina with rare exceptions, but there's a good left and a bad left. The good left is Garcia and Lula, and then there's the bad left, which is Chavez, Morales, maybe Correa. And that's the split.

In order to maintain that position, it's necessary to resort to some fancy footwork. For example, it's necessary not to report the fact that when Lula was re-elected in October, his foreign trip and one of his first acts was to visit Caracas to support Chavez and his electoral campaign and to dedicate a joint Venezuelan-Brazilian project on the Orinoco River, to talk about new projects and so on. It's necessary not to report the fact that a couple of weeks later in Cochabamba, Bolivia, which is the heart of the bad guys, there was a meeting of all South American leaders. There had been bad blood between Chavez and Garcia, but it was apparently patched up. They laid plans for pretty constructive South American integration, but that just doesn't fit the US agenda. So it wasn't reported.

How is the political deadlock in Lebanon impacting on the US government's decision to potentially go to war with Iran? Is there a relationship at all?

There's a relationship. I presume part of the reason for the US-Israel invasion of Lebanon in July – and it is US-Israeli, the Lebanese are correct in calling it that – part of the reason I suppose was that Hezbollah is considered a deterrent to a potential US-Israeli attack on Iran. It had a deterrent capacity, i.e. rockets. And the goal I presume was to wipe out the deterrent so as to free up the United States and Israel for an eventual attack on Iran. That's at least part of the reason. The official reason given for the invasion can't be taken seriously for a moment. That's the capture of two Israeli soldiers and the killing of a couple of others. For decades Israel has been capturing and kidnapping Lebanese and Palestinian refugees on the high seas, from Cyprus to Lebanon, killing them in Lebanon, bringing them to Israel, holding them as hostages. It's been going on for decades. Has anybody called for an invasion of Israel?

Of course Israel doesn't want any competition in the region. But there's no principled basis for the massive attack on Lebanon, which was horrendous. In fact, one of the last acts of the US-Israeli invasion, right after the ceasefire was announced before it was implemented, was to saturate much of the south with cluster bombs.

There's no military purpose for that, the war was over, the ceasefire was coming.

UN de-mining groups that are working there say that the scale is unprecedented. It's much worse than any other place they've worked: Kosovo, Afghanistan, Iraq, anywhere. There are supposed to be about one million bomblets left there. A large percentage of them don't explode until you pick them up, a child picks them up, or a farmer hits it with a hoe or something. So what it does basically is make the south uninhabitable until the mining teams, for which the United States and Israel don't contribute, clean it up. This is arable land. It means that farmers can't go back; it means that it may undermine a potential Hezbollah deterrent. They apparently have pretty much withdrawn from the south, according to the UN.

You can't mention Hezbollah in the US media without putting in the context of 'Iranian-supported Hezbollah'. That's its name. Its name is Iranian-supported Hezbollah. It gets Iranian support. But you can mention Israel without saying US-supported Israel. So this is more tacit propaganda. The idea that Hezbollah is acting as an agent of Iran is very dubious. It's not accepted by specialists on Iran or specialists on Hezbollah. But it's the party line. Or sometimes you can put in Syria, i.e. 'Syrian-supported Hezbollah', but since Syria is of less interest now you have to emphasise Iranian support.

How can the US government think an attack on Iran is feasible given troop availability, troop capacity, and public sentiment?

As far as I'm aware, the military in the United States thinks it's crazy. And from whatever leaks we have from intelligence, the intelligence community thinks it's outlandish, but not impossible. If you look at people who have really been involved in the Pentagon's strategic planning for years, people like Sam Gardiner, they point out that there are things that possibly could be done.

I don't think any of the outside commentators, at least as far as I'm aware, have taken very seriously the idea of bombing nuclear facilities. They say if there will be bombing it'll be carpet bombing. So get the nuclear facilities but get the rest of the country, too, with an exception. By accident of geography, the world's major oil resources are in Shi'ite-dominated areas. Iran's oil is concentrated right near the Gulf, which happens to be an Arab area, not Persian. Khuzestan is Arab, has been loyal to Iran, fought with Iran not Iraq during the Iran-Iraq war. This is a potential source of dissension. I would be amazed if there isn't an attempt going on to stir up secessionist elements in Khuzestan. US forces right across the border in Iraq, including the surge, are available potentially to 'defend' an independent Khuzestan against Iran, which is the way it would be put, if they can carry it off.

Do you think that's what the surge was for?

That's one possibility. There was a release of a Pentagon war-gaming report, in December 2004, with Gardiner leading it. It was released and published in the *Atlantic Monthly*. They couldn't come up with a proposal that didn't lead to disaster, but one of the things they considered was maintaining troop presence in Iraq beyond what's to be used in Iraq for troop replacement and so on, and use them for a potential land move in Iran – presumably Khuzestan where the oil is. If you could carry that off, you could just bomb the rest of the country to dust.

Again, I would be amazed if there aren't efforts to sponsor secessionist movements elsewhere, among the Azeri population for example. It's a very complex ethnic mix in Iran; much of the population isn't Persian. There are secessionist tendencies anyway and almost certainly, without knowing any of the facts, the United States is trying to stir them up, to break the country internally if possible. The strategy appears to be: try to break the country up internally, try to impel the leadership to be as harsh and brutal as possible.

That's the immediate consequence of constant threats. Everyone knows that. That's one of the reasons the reformists, Shirin Ebadi and Akbar Ganji and others, are bitterly complaining about the US threats, that it's undermining their efforts to reform and democratise Iran. But that's presumably its purpose. Since it's an obvious consequence you have to assume it's the purpose. Just like in law, anticipated consequences are taken as the evidence for intention. And here it's so obvious you can't seriously doubt it.

So it could be that one strain of the policy is to stir up secessionist movements, particularly in the oil rich regions, the Arab regions near the Gulf, also the Azeri regions and others. Second is to try to get the leadership to be as brutal and harsh and repressive as possible, to stir up internal disorder and maybe resistance. And a third is to try to pressure other countries, and Europe is the most amenable, to join efforts to strangle Iran economically. Europe is kind of dragging its feet but they usually go along with the United States.

The efforts to intensify the harshness of the regime show up in many ways. For example, the West absolutely adores Ahmadinejad. Any wild statement that he comes out with immediately gets circulated in headlines and mis-translated. They love him. But anybody who knows anything about Iran, presumably the editorial offices, knows that he doesn't have anything to do with foreign policy. Foreign policy is in the hands of his superior, the Supreme Leader Khamenei. But they don't report his statements, particularly when his statements are pretty conciliatory. For example, they love when Ahmadinejad says that Israel shouldn't exist, but they don't like it when Khamenei right afterwards says that Iran supports the Arab League position on Israel-Palestine. As far as I'm aware, it never got reported. Actually you could find Khamenei's more conciliatory positions in the *Financial Times*, but not here. And it's repeated by Iranian diplomats, but that's no good. The Arab League proposal calls for normalisation of relations with Israel if it accepts the international consensus of the two-state settlement which has been blocked by the United States and Israel for thirty years. And that's not a good story, so it's either not mentioned or it's hidden somewhere.

It's very hard to predict the Bush administration today because they're deeply irrational. They were irrational to start with but now they're desperate. They have created an unimaginable catastrophe in Iraq. This should've been one of the easiest military occupations in history and they succeeded in turning it into one of the worst military disasters in history. They can't control it and it's almost impossible for them to get out for reasons you can't discuss in the United States, because to discuss the reasons why they can't get out would be to concede the reasons why they invaded.

We're supposed to believe that oil had nothing to do with it, that if Iraq were exporting pickles or jelly and the centre of world oil production were in the South Pacific, that the United States would've liberated them anyway. It has nothing to do with the oil – what a crass idea. Anyone with their head screwed on knows that that can't be true. Allowing an independent and sovereign Iraq could be a nightmare for the United States. It would mean that it would be Shi'ite-dominated, at least if it's minimally democratic. It would continue to improve relations with Iran – just what the United States doesn't want to see. And beyond that, right across the border in Saudi Arabia where most of Saudi oil is, there happens to be a large Shi'ite population, probably a majority.

Moves towards sovereignty in Iraq stimulate pressures first for human rights among the bitterly repressed Shi'ite population but also towards some degree of autonomy. You can imagine a kind of a loose Shi'ite alliance in Iraq, Saudi Arabia, and Iran, controlling most of the world's oil and independent of the United States. And much worse, although Europe can be intimidated by the United States, China can't. It's one of the reasons, the main reasons, why China is considered a threat. We're back to the Mafia principle.

China has been there for 3,000 years, has contempt for the barbarians, is overcoming a century of domination, and simply moves on its own. It does not get intimidated when Uncle Sam shakes his fist. That's scary. In particular, it's dangerous in the case of the Middle East. China is the centre of the Asian energy security grid, which includes the Central Asian states and Russia. India is also hovering around the edge, South Korea is involved, and Iran is an associate member of some kind. If the Middle East oil resources around the Gulf, which are the main ones in the world, if they link up to the Asian grid, the United States is really a second-rate power. A lot is at stake in not withdrawing from Iraq.

I'm sure that these issues are discussed in internal planning. It's inconceivable that they can't think of this. But it's out of public discussion, it's not in the media, it's not in the journals, it's not in the Baker-Hamilton report. And I think you can understand the reason. To bring up these issues would open the question why the United States and Britain invaded. And that question is taboo.

It's a principle that anything our leaders do is for noble reasons. It may be mistaken, it may be ugly, but basically noble. And if you bring in normal, moderate, conservative, strategic, economic objectives you threaten that principle. It's remarkable the extent to which it's held. So the original pretexts for the invasion were weapons of mass destruction and ties to al Qaeda that nobody but maybe Wolfowitz or Cheney took seriously. The single question, as they kept reiterating in the leadership, was: will Saddam give up his programmes of weapons of mass destruction? The single question was answered a couple of months later, the wrong way. And quickly the party line shifted. In November 2003, Bush announced his freedom agenda: our real goal is to bring democracy to Iraq, to transform the Middle East. That became the party line, instantly.

But it's a mistake to pick out individuals because it's close to universal, even in scholarship. In fact you can even find scholarly articles that begin by giving the evidence that it's complete farce but nevertheless accept it. There was a pretty good study of the freedom agenda in *Current History* by two scholars and they give the facts. They point out that the freedom agenda was announced on November 2003 after the failure to find weapons of mass destruction, but the freedom agenda is real even if there's no evidence for it.

In fact, if you look at our policies they're the opposite. Take Palestine. There was a free election in Palestine, but it came out the wrong way. So instantly, the United States and Israel with Europe tagging along, moved to punish the Palestinian people, and punish them harshly, because they voted the wrong way in a free election. That's accepted here in the West as perfectly normal. That illustrates the deep hatred and contempt for democracy among western élites, so deep-seated they can't even perceive it when it's in front of their eyes. You punish people severely if they vote the wrong way in a free election. There's a pretext for that too, repeated every day: Hamas must agree to first recognise Israel, second to end all violence, third to accept past agreements. Try to find a mention of the fact that the United States and Israel reject all three of those. They obviously don't recognise Palestine, they certainly don't withdraw the use of violence or the threat of it – in fact they insist on it – and they don't accept past agreements, including the road map.

I suspect one of the reasons why Jimmy Carter's book has come under such fierce attack is because it's the first time, I think, in the mainstream, that one can find the truth about the road map. I have never seen anything in the mainstream that discusses the fact that Israel instantly rejected the road map with US support. They formally accepted it but added 14 reservations that totally eviscerated it. It was done instantly. It's public knowledge, I've written about it, talked about it, so have others, but I've never seen it mentioned in the mainstream before. And obviously they don't accept the Arab League proposal or any other serious proposal. In fact they've been blocking the international consensus on the two-state solution for decades. But Hamas has to accept them.

It really makes no sense. Hamas is a political party and political parties don't recognise other countries. And Hamas itself has made it very clear – they actually carried out a truce for a year and a half, didn't respond to Israeli attacks, and have called for a long-term truce, during which it'd be possible to negotiate a settlement along the lines of the international consensus and the Arab League proposal.

All of this is obvious, it's right on the surface, and that's just one example of the deep hatred of democracy on the part of western élites. It's a striking example but you can add case after case. Yet, the president announced the freedom agenda and if the dear leader said something, it's got to be true, kind of North Korean style. Therefore there's a freedom agenda even if there's a mountain of evidence against it, the only evidence for it is in words, even apart from the timing.

In the 2008 presidential election, how will the candidates approach Iran? Do you think Iran will be a deciding factor in the elections?

What they're saying so far is not encouraging. I still think, despite everything, that the US is very unlikely to attack Iran. It could be a huge catastrophe; nobody knows what the consequences would be. I imagine that only an administration that's really desperate would resort to that. But if the Democratic candidates are on the verge of winning the election, the administration is going to be desperate. It still has the problem of Iraq: can't stay in, and can't get out.

The Senate Democrats can't seem to achieve consensus on this issue.

I think there's a reason for it. The reason is just thinking through the consequences of allowing an independent, partially democratic Iraq. The consequences are non-trivial. We may decide to hide our heads in the sand and pretend we can't think it through because we cannot allow the question of why the United States invaded to open, but that's very self-destructive.

Is there any connection to this conversation and why we cannot find the political will and momentum to enact legislation that would reduce $C0_2$ emissions levels, institute a cap-and-trade system, etc.?

It's perfectly clear why the United States didn't sign the Kyoto Protocol. Again, there's overwhelming popular support for signing, in fact it's so strong that a majority of Bush voters in 2004 thought that he was in favour of the Kyoto Protocol. It's such an obvious thing to support. Popular support for alternative energy has been very high for years. But it harms corporate profits. After all, that's the administration's constituency.

I remember talking to, 40 years ago, one of the leading people in the government who was involved in arms control, pressing for arms control measures, détente, and so on. He's very high up, and we were talking about whether arms control could succeed. And only partially as a joke he said, 'Well it might succeed if the high tech industry makes more profit from arms control than it can make from weapons-related research and production. If we get to that tipping point maybe arms control will work'. He was partially joking but there's a truth that lies behind it.

How do we move forward on climate change without beggaring the south?

Unfortunately, the poor countries, the south, are going to suffer the worst according to most projections – and that being so, it undermines support in the north for doing much. Look at the ozone story. As long as it was the southern hemisphere that was being threatened, there was very little talk about it. When it was discovered in the north, very quickly actions were taken to do something about it. Right now there's discussion of putting serious effort into developing a malaria vaccine, because global warming might extend malaria to the rich countries, so something should be done about it.

Same thing on health insurance. Here's an issue where, for the general population, it's been the leading domestic issue, or close to it, for years. And there's a consensus for a national healthcare system on the model of other industrial countries, maybe expanding Medicare to everyone or something like that. Well, that's off the agenda, nobody can talk about that. The insurance companies don't like it, the financial industry doesn't like it and so on.

Now there's a change taking place. What's happening is that manufacturing industries are beginning to turn to support for it because they're being undermined by the hopelessly inefficient US healthcare system. It's the worst in the industrial world by far, and they have to pay for it. Since it's employer-compensated, in part, their production costs are much higher than those competitors who have a national healthcare system. Take GM. If it produces the same car in Detroit and in Windsor across the border in Canada, it saves, I forget the number, I think over $1000 with the Windsor production because there's a national healthcare system. It's much more efficient, it's much cheaper, it's much more effective.

So the manufacturing industry is starting to press for some kind of national healthcare. Now it's beginning to put it on the agenda. It doesn't matter if the population wants it. What 90 per cent of the population wants would be kind of irrelevant. But if part of the concentration of corporate capital that basically runs the country – another thing we're not allowed to say, but it's obvious – if part of that sector becomes in favour then the issue moves onto the political agenda.

So how does the south get its voice heard on the international agenda? Is the World Social Forum a place for it?

The World Social Forum is very important but of course that can't be covered in the West. In fact, I remember reading an article, I think in the *Financial Times*, about the two major forums that were taking place. One was the World Economic Forum in Davos and a second was a forum in Herzeliyah in Israel, a right wing forum in Herzeliyah. Those were the two forums. Of course there was also the World Social Forum in Nairobi, but that's only tens of thousands of people from around the world.

With the trend towards vilifying the G77 at the UN one wonders where the developing world can effectively voice their concerns.

The developing world voice can be amplified enormously by support from the wealthy and the privileged, otherwise it's very likely to be marginalised, as in every other issue.

So it's up to us.

* * *

This interview was first published in Foreign Policy in Focus (www.fpif.org).

Speaking Peace on the BBC

Craig Murray

I had the interesting experience of sitting on set at BBC News 24 for over an hour on 5 April, intermittently talking and intermittently on camera. I had come in to discuss both the maritime boundaries issue and the question of the behind the scenes diplomatic negotiations. As Oliver Miles said, there were at least ten bilateral discussions between Iran and British ambassadors, ministers and No 10 officials. Tony Blair might claim there were no negotiations, but they weren't discussing the weather.

Anyway, I was on air when the hostages arrived by helicopter and were reunited with their families. Thus I found myself being asked for an hour questions such as 'How do you think the families are feeling?'

I should say that the presenters were really nice, and the hectic atmosphere of a newsroom on a big live breaking story is great fun. I found myself involved in an interesting game of offering deadpan expert analysis, but interspersing it with subversive comment. I didn't want to push that too hard or I was pretty plain I would have got yanked off. So over the course of an hour I first slipped in the observation that, as a taxpayer, I was not too keen on financing very expensive warships steaming around the Gulf allegedly to collect vehicle excise duty. Later I was able to say that, while I shared the unalloyed delight at the return of the 15, I was thinking rather more about the families of the four British servicemen who had been killed in Iraq that day, and their civilian interpreter. Before they could recover from the shock of that burst through the reverential coverage, I added the 70 Iraqi civilians who on average die every day.

You should understand that over the long broadcast I mostly talked about the return of the captives and had no difficulty in being genuinely upbeat and happy about that. But the reunion of captives and families probably had the largest live news audience for many months;

Craig Murray was the United Kingdom's Ambassador to Uzbekistan until 2004, when he was removed for complaining about torture in that country. He is the author of Murder in Samarkand *(Mainstream Publishing).*

it did not escape the No 10 spin doctors' attention that their 'Triumph for Tony' moment was being jeopardised by a dissident having been allowed on the BBC.

Ask yourself – when is the last time you saw an anti-war voice, as opposed to a pro-war 'military' or 'security' expert, asked by the BBC to comment on a Middle East development? Yet the majority of people in this country are against the war. If they want an ex-diplomat, they go for pro-war cheerleaders Pauline Neville Jones or Christopher Meyer, even though eight out of ten ex-British Ambassadors are against the war.

Anyway the outraged phone calls from the government to the BBC started coming in. As a result, having been introduced as 'Former Head of the Foreign Office Maritime Section and Former British Ambassador...' the first time, I was reintroduced as 'Craig Murray, who was sacked as British Ambassador to Uzbekistan for opposing British government policy'. The poor presenters, with whom I had been getting on well for an hour, seemed embarrassed.

I therefore decided the gloves were off, and introduced 'the elephant in the room – that the large majority of the British people don't believe that our servicemen should be in Iraq and in harm's way in the first place.'

There is no doubt at all that when you make anti-war or anti-government points on the BBC the whole body language and line of questioning indicates that you are some sort of isolated extremist. Of course, our so-called opposition parties fail to make any such points, and the BBC's normal pool of experts are hand-picked to be reliably right wing on these issues. The absolutely astonishing thing is that I then whizzed off to Sky News (Fox affiliate) and there, in the heart of the Murdoch Empire, the atmosphere is totally different.

I was asked open questions if anything leading me on to be overtly critical of the war, Tony Blair and John Bolton. This is not unusual. Tony Benn, George Galloway and I all get far easier access to Sky than the BBC. Sky does seem to maintain a modicum of journalistic integrity. The BBC has totally lost it since Gilligan, Dyke and Hussey were sacked for telling the truth about Iraqi WMD, and David Kelly was murdered.

Anyway, after Sky I went to buy a birthday present for Nadira. A lady outside the shop told me that she had just seen me on the TV. 'I used to listen to you on Radio 4' she said, 'You looked a lot better on the radio.'

THE BERTRAND RUSSELL PEACE FOUNDATION

DOSSIER

2007 Number 24

NO MORE HIROSHIMAS!

The 2007 World Conference against Atomic and Hydrogen Bombs will be held from 3 to 9 August 2007 in the A-bombed cities of Hiroshima and Nagasaki with the theme 'For a Nuclear Weapon-Free, Peaceful and Just World'. We cordially invite all those people in the world as well as Japan who wish to contribute to achieving this goal through interaction, cooperation, and solidarity to take part in and support the 2007 World Conference.

The Iraq war was launched based on lies about weapons of mass destruction being developed by Iraq, and it is now a quagmire of death. The Bush Administration is now under severe criticism both at home and internationally.

Amid growing concern over the danger of nuclear proliferation, calls for the abolition of nuclear weapons are increasing. Recently, former US Secretary of State Henry A. Kissinger and other former key US administration officials proposed that a 'world without nuclear weapons' should be created and for this 'a major effort should be launched by the United States', which 'would lend additional weight to efforts already under way to solve the problem of nuclear proliferation'.

The Bush Administration insists on modernising its nuclear armaments and is clinging to the policy of the possible use of nuclear weapons. It is also insisting on continuing the Iraq war. However, such a policy will only lead to deeper isolation and total failure. We will work to increase people's movements to make the 21st century free of the threat of nuclear weapons and wars at the earliest possible time.

The efforts by the Japanese anti-nuclear peace movement are drawing attention from people around the world, thus raising their hopes. The recent development on the issue of North Korea's nuclear programmes can be a concrete step forward toward its peaceful resolution. We do not condone the emergence of new nuclear weapons-possessing countries. We stand firm against the Japanese government considering arguments for arming Japan with nuclear weapons by capitalising on the issue of North Korea's nuclear programme. We oppose Japan's dependence on the US 'nuclear umbrella' as well as its attempt to push ahead with the adverse revision of the Japanese Constitution.

Japan is the atomic bombed country with its 'Article 9' and its Three Non-Nuclear Principles. We will increase efforts to transform our country into one that will contribute to creating a peaceful world without nuclear weapons.

The World Conference against A & H Bombs, working together with the *Hibakusha* (A-bomb survivors), has played a major role in advancing the anti-nuclear movement worldwide. In recent years, it has helped develop international solidarity and cooperation between non-governmental organisations and national governments that are making efforts to abolish nuclear weapons. This has had a positive impact on international politics. By making the voices of the *Hibakusha* and other nuclear victims heard around the world, we will work to increase the current of calls for the swift abolition of nuclear weapons. We sincerely hope that the 2007 World Conference against A & H Bombs will further build on our past achievements involving young people bearing the future of humanity and the broad range of people from around the world as well as Japan. With this, we cordially call on you to take part in and give support to the World Conference, and to cooperate with us in the various activities in preparation for a successful World Conference.

Contact the Japan Council Against A & H Bombs for more information (antiatom@topaz.plala.or.jp).

BLAIR PROSECUTION AT THE INTERNATIONAL CRIMINAL COURT?

Luis Moreno-Ocampo, the International Criminal Court's chief prosecutor, has urged Arab countries, particularly Iraq, to sign up to the Court to enable allegations against the West to be pursued. He said it was still possible for an investigation to be launched into coalition actions in Iraq if that country signed up. Iraq's ambassador to the United Nations, Hamid al-Bayati, said that his country was actively considering doing so.

Mr Moreno-Ocampo said it was frustrating that the Court was viewed in the Arab world as biased in favour of the West. Asked by a British newspaper, *The Sunday Telegraph* (18 March 2007), whether he could envisage a situation in which Mr Blair and Mr Bush found themselves in the dock answering charges of war crimes in Iraq, he replied: 'Of course, that could be a possibility … whatever country joins the Court can know that whoever commits a crime in their country could be prosecuted by me'.

America has refused to accept the Court's jurisdiction and has signed more than a hundred separate bi-lateral agreements with other states not to hand over its citizens to the Court. Britain, however, has signed up.

Sudan, which has been investigated by the Court over its role in the killing of civilians in Darfur, has called for the International Criminal Court to investigate coalition actions in Iraq, although it is not a signatory to the Rome agreement which established the Court.

The UN Security Council can ask the Court to act – as in the case of Darfur – or the Court can launch an investigation if it receives a complaint from a state which is party to the Rome agreement. It can also look into alleged offences carried out by, or on the territory of, a party to the agreement.

Reviews

March On

Ann Pettitt, *Walking to Greenham: How the Peace-camp began and the Cold War ended*, Honno (www.honno.co.uk), 320 pages, paperback ISBN 1 870206 76 2, £8.99

Peace March 1981, or *Fredsmarsjen 1981,* to give it its original, Norwegian title, did not end in Paris on 6 August, after six weeks on the road from Copenhagen. It merely paused for breath, resting its weary feet, searching for someone like Ann Pettitt to take up the torch and carry it on. Later that same month, Ann and her friends set out from Cardiff for the gates of Greenham Common. The rest, as they say, is history.

Part One of Ann Pettitt's autobiography tells the story:

> '… I was trying to help write a leaflet in someone's house in Kidwelly, about nuclear-free zones. I was feeling bored and stuck generally … what was the point of your local town declaring itself a "nuclear-free zone" when what we were facing was the possibility of a nuclear war "limited" to Europe? My eye caught an item in a *Peace News* magazine that was lying open on the floor, about a group of women walking from Copenhagen to Paris to protest about this threat. I no longer felt bored or stuck. I felt terribly excited.'

Ann and a handful of other women in Wales set about organising their follow-on march. Caring for children, gardening, and all their other responsibilities had to be managed at the same time as they looked for places to stay, begged money, and gathered the vitals to sustain what became Women for Life on Earth.

Twenty and more years on, what was achieved, and why did Ann Pettitt do it? The short answer to the first question is rather startling: the end of the Cold War and the removal of some 'theatre' nuclear weapons from Europe. Ann has her own particular perspective on that sea change in world affairs. From Greenham she had journeyed to the Soviet Union to meet with members of the unofficial Moscow Group for Trust. She, together with a British and an American colleague, wished to discuss the Group's 'Appeal to Governments and Publics', which called for greater mutual trust between peoples East and West based on direct contact.

Subsequently, in the company of Dr. Olga Medvedkova from the Moscow Group, the Greenham delegation visited the official Soviet Peace Committee. The protests at Greenham Common were big news in the Soviet Union, where they were portrayed as directed against aggressive US militarism. But the Peace Committee hierarchy was unimpressed at Dr Medvedkova's inclusion in the delegation which brought first-hand news from Britain. She was subsequently arrested and convicted on a trumped-up charge, but given a suspended sentence, indicating some belated sensitivity to wider international opinion.

Mikhail Gorbachev, then a comparatively unknown Politburo member, surprised a visiting delegation from the British Communist Party 'by describing the provocative behaviour of someone called Ann Pettitt who had visited with a Greenham "delegation" and had brought an uninvited person into an official meeting.' Gorbachev suggested to the assembled delegation that they should keep their peace movement comrades 'under better disciplinary control'.

Notwithstanding her personal notoriety, Ann Pettitt identifies Gorbachev as the man who broke the mould, and moved the world away from gathering confrontation and towards serial disarmament measures which encompassed the removal of cruise missiles from Greenham and, ultimately, the return of at least part of the base to common land. He 'led the world out of the arms race … a wise and honest leader, astonishingly undervalued' by his own people.

Why did Ann answer the call of the Scandinavian women and keep marching for a Europe free of nuclear weapons? A deeper motivation seems to have been at work, borne of her parent's wartime experiences in Northern France and, in particular, her father's enthusiasm for the Soviet Union, which led him to make an unauthorised visit to Moscow in 1937. The person Colin had come to see had mysteriously disappeared. The implication is that he had disappeared in Stalin's purges of the 1930s which engulfed millions of Soviet citizens. Six years later, in 1943, Solange, Ann's mother-to-be, would taunt German guards in the northern French town of Tourcoing with cries of 'Stalingrad', as news spread of the Germans' defeat there. The parents' commitments and courage found their own particular echo in the daughter.

Ann Pettitt says she can't quite remember how the Cold War ended. But she has given us a poignant and insightful account of the bits she can recall, which resonates strongly with the assault on life and liberty that is now our daily lot.

Tony Simpson

Pictures and Poetry

Bertolt Brecht, *War Primer*, translated and edited by John Willett, Libris, 196 pages, ISBN 9 781870 352468, £19.95

During his exile from Germany during the Second World War, Brecht cut out war photographs from newspapers and magazines, kept them in a portfolio, and wrote four line poems to accompany them. We reproduce three of the pages in his *War Primer* by kind permission of the publishers.

The Nazi Big Three—Their Ending Should Be Wagnerian.

O swan-song! 'Never seek to question me!'
O pilgrims' choir! O fiery-magic trick!
Song of the Rhine gold on an empty belly!
That's what I'd call the Bayreuth Republic.

Field Marshal Fedor von Beck

Field Marshal Hugo Sperrle

Field Marshal Karl von Rundstedt

Field Marshal Erwin Rommel

General Heinz Guderian

Field Marshal Siegmund List

Here are six murderers. Now don't turn away
And don't just nod and murmur 'That's the truth'.
Showing them up has cost us to this day
Fifty great cities and most of our youth.

Look at the helmets of the vanquished! Yet
Surely the moment when we came undone
Was not when they were smitten from our heads
But when we first agreed to put them on.

Burning Hot

George Monbiot, *Heat: How to Stop the Planet Burning,* Allen Lane, 277pages, hardback ISBN 978-0713999235, £17.99

George Monbiot has for many years been both a key voice of political dissent and an espouser of practical solutions for challenging the inherent structural inequalities of national and global power. Presciently, it is with his environmental campaigning, and specifically that most omnipresent of subjects, climate change, that his latest clarion call of a book is concerned. In his own words, it is a 'manifesto for action'.

The thrust of the argument is relatively simple: we have perhaps about 25 years to reduce our output of CO_2 and other greenhouse gases by 60 per cent globally. This means that through accepted 'contraction and convergence' criteria the advanced industrialised world's reduction has to be of the order of 90 per cent, the United Kingdom included. This book is a national blueprint setting out how to achieve that target. He is persuaded that alternatively, with a 'business as usual' scenario, or weak palliatives, there is a high probability that we will reach a global tipping point, where runaway natural forces lead to incalculable effects. Monbiot is convinced that we need to stabilise at 450 parts per million (ppm) CO_2 (plus the other greenhouse gases) by 2030 to prevent temperatures rising above the 2°C threshold. As a comparison, Sir Nicholas Stern, in his recent Review on the Economics of Climate Change, uses a broader stabilisation range of 500 to 550ppm by 2050, and thinks that 'stabilisation at 450ppm CO_2 is already almost out of reach'. Even Stern's more leisurely containment, he admits, puts us within the possibility of a 4.5°C warming, dangerously close to the Permian extinction temperature of a 6°C rise when 95% of living organisms met their demise. Monbiot, on the other hand, is confident that meeting the target of no more than 2°C will make 'the sort of warming that took place at the end of the Permian impossible'. (If you remain unconvinced of the immediacy of the problem, then Fred Pearce's book *The Last Generation* is a readable introduction to the science of climate change and the debates within the climatological community.)

Monbiot's book contains, as one would expect, a fair amount of scientific calculation of possibilities and likely scenarios, and the reader must be prepared for this. If you are looking for science with 100 per cent assured outcomes you will be disappointed, but this does not mean that there is not a large scientific consensus that global warming caused by anthropogenic industrial sources is happening. There is much scientific debate over differing climate models and the rapidity of change but a virtually total scientific consensus with regard to direction. This is inspite of the devious activities of the 'denial industry' to muddy the waters, succinctly exposed in chapter two of Monbiot's book. And what a repugnant band of apostates they make: ranging from those media pump attendants of denial, Melanie Phillips and Peter Hitchens, through Internet obfuscation placed by bogus academic and 'grassroots' citizen organisations whose funding apparently derives from those paragons of corporate rectitude, Exxon and Phillip Morris. New support for denial has recently surfaced in the European Parliament from recently joined East European countries, among them the Lithuanian Free Market Institute, funded by a large petrol company Mazeikiu Nafta and Phillip Morris *(www.Corpwatch 22/02/07)*. The only recycling this lot go in for is of their own spurious science.

Monbiot's solution proposes combining a number of measures: carbon rationing; an adaptation of existing power generation technologies through underground carbon sequestration; a localised energy internet with home and area-based power and heating units using a mixture of renewable, hydrogen and natural gas generation techniques; the deployment of geographically appropriate renewable solar and wind energy; a massive improvement in housing energy insulation efficiency; major reductions in individualised transport systems, namely the car, and the substitution of a much improved motorway coach system; the rationalising of retail and wholesale distribution; and a sweeping reduction in mass air travel. There will be a place for the market but it will be largely confined to realistic carbon pricing, and he rejects carbon taxing for its rightly perceived regressive nature. He proposes a carbon rationing system that would give an equal carbon allowance to each citizen and could be traded to give an element of consumer choice and yet still, hopefully, reflect individual social and medical needs. This proposal, potentially still to a degree favouring the wealthy, has already been mooted in New Labour circles by David Miliband.

In contrast Monbiot rightly sees 'carbon offsetting' as at best akin to medieval indulgences, a sop to the conscience preventing the tackling of the real problem, giving no worthwhile reduction and, at worst, an unregulated arena for dubious entrepreneurs, and even capable of inflicting bad science and environmental practice on mainly Third World communities. Carbon trading through the present European Union emission scheme is, as presently constituted, a 'classic act of enclosure' with rights and subsidies dispensed to the big corporations instead of to the population as a whole. Additionally, as Monbiot rightly points out, the Kyoto and European Union emission stipulations were always well padded in favour of the industrial corporations and nations who should have scant difficulties in meeting the targets, given the added bonus of purchasing the emission deficits of the collapsed industrial base of the ex-Soviet economies. For that matter what Bush objected to about the Kyoto agreement was not the specified lax parameters on emissions themselves, but the principle of the national restriction on the United States' right to pollute and the dangers of an on-going process of negotiated 'constriction and convergence'. Monbiot is only too well aware of the dangers of applying marketplace solutions to what Stern has called 'the greatest and widest-ranging market failure ever seen'.

Literally grasping at straws, the US government in particular seems to think that a way out of its climate impasse is through bio-fuels. (This would have the added advantage of loosening the market grip of those troublesome oil-rich states.) Consequently, Brazil with its sugar cane-sourced cheap ethanol industry, based on staggering levels of human exploitation *(Guardian 09/03/07)*, appears to be succumbing to Bush's deadly embrace. This conflicts with the interests of the

US farming belt, already beginning to exploit its commercially more expensive bio-fuel crops at the expense of food production, both in terms of availability and price. In fact the major difficulty with this solution is the stress it will put on global food crop production. Monbiot, for example, maintains that there are 5.7 million hectares of arable land in the United Kingdom and that the production of bio-fuels for one year just for 'cars, buses and lorries would require 25.9 million hectares'. Bio-fuels have some useful applications, but not at the expense of global food supply, gross human exploitation, and deforestation of rainforests with the consequent rainfall depletion.

Neither is the solution to be found in the tokenism of Blair's Caribbean holiday flight carbon offsets and Cameron's bicycling toy chimney windmill gestures. Nor does Monbiot accept the necessity for the hair-shirt back-to-nature approach of a biogas energy system driven by our own ordure or living in a yurt somewhere on Salisbury Plain — his are eminently practical if daunting proposals. However, when you perceive the mountain to be climbed when we have not yet managed to scramble over the foothills of ever more eminent political rhetoric, it does seem bleak. As Monbiot remarks it 'is not that people aren't hearing … but that they don't want to know'. The most noticeable effects of global warming are often to be felt in the developing world, impacting on their poorest communities, who are usually the least responsible in terms of emissions. As with the global consequences of other manifestations of the neo-liberal world economy, even in the heartland of neo-liberalist capitalism, it is the poor, the elderly, the sick, the very young and the ethnic minorities who suffer the derelictions of the state at times of crisis, as we saw most graphically in New Orleans (2005) and the European heat wave (2003).

Hardly a day goes by without some new proclamation on the importance of halting climate change from the great and the not-so-good. Meanwhile, ever greater coats of 'greenwash' attempt to seduce us with the idea that BP, Walmart and Marks & Spencer are to save the planet. As Monbiot notes, just to get the latter supermarkets to fit doors to all their refrigerators so as not to be in a perpetual energy war with their own heating systems would appear to be too much to ask. At the same time, the New Labour Government steams ahead with airport expansion, places niggardly financial limits on grants for renewable energy initiatives, obstructs environmental legislation within the European Union, funds motorway lane expansion, gives support to nuclear power expansion, and who can now remember John Prescott's 'public transport Renaissance' that never happened? The car corporations all have their prototype 'green' cars, but ask them to restrict new mass-market cars to 120 kg/km carbon emissions and the whines of protest from BMW and Volkswagen are sufficient to force a climbdown by the European Commission.

Unlike Blair, Monbiot places nuclear power generation second from the bottom when it comes to desirable power sources, the very bottom being open-cast coal mining. He admits that the figures for nuclear power can be manipulated by both supporters and detractors to support their case, but makes a powerful case himself for its non-expansion. This he bases on the familiar arguments of waste storage, weapons production, terrorism, the industry's historical record and an energy-based input/output analysis. Alongside the expansion of renewables, electricity generation should at least, in the relatively short term, as a 'partial solution', continue to use natural gas but with the carbon emissions sequestered in suitable geological sites. Like many environmentalists he fears a return to relatively cheap coal when the oil and gas start to run out.

Throughout the book Monbiot, where possible, has made every effort to cost his proposals and compare them against alternatives, a testament to the hard work he and his small band of researchers have put into the book. But whatever way you look at the problem, the infrastructural costs to make many of Monbiot's ideas work will be colossal. We perhaps forget that the change from wood burning to coal took perhaps 200 years of development. Add to that a further 100 years for the full infrastructural development of oil-based technology and it seems, in retrospect, a fairly leisurely pace of transformation. In contrast, we need to make the transition to renewables and possibly hydrogen in a couple decades at the most, according to Monbiot's scenario. He suggests therefore a mixture of technologies and scales of action. As well as relatively immediate solutions there are also suggestions for long-term endeavours. For example, it may be possible to develop a new long distance international electrical power grid based on DC (direct current) transmission sourced from enormous solar farms based in the Sahara. Many of his more long-term proposals in particular need changes to the national and international economic infrastructure and call for a degree of planning and coordination of gargantuan proportions. The book to some extent downplays the enormity of the changes required and does not touch on the many and significant political and economic obstacles, but in Monbiot's defence this is not the book's purpose. We do need practical plans to meet the technical problems but also, perhaps more importantly, practical conceptions for focusing and building a mass movement across the radical political spectrum, capable of providing the necessary leverage.

Appropriately each chapter of the book is introduced with a pithy quote from Christopher Marlowe's play *Doctor Faustus* to set the scene for our 'live now pay later' pact with fossil fuels. But moderate as they seem, Monbiot's proposals would alter the whole emphasis and practice of the retail trade, with consumerist choices inevitably becoming much narrower. The compensations wedding workers in the industrial nations to market capitalism would become increasingly tenuous: the car, the cheap holiday flights, even the 'retail therapy' visits to Tesco and M&S, should you be so inclined, would be brought into question by the necessary redefinition of transport and material distribution. Implicitly, reasonable as Monbiot's schema appears, ultimately it demands a new relationship between peoples, nations and between Man and Nature. It is now far too late to continue with capitalism's Hobbesian, business-as-usual war on nature, whatever the many difficulties of forging an alternative.

History is not packed with occasions where definitive action is taken without the actuality of extreme need and, whilst capitalism has the ability to plan, it is usually to assist relatively short-term accumulation, not generalised social need. Monbiot's plan (whilst not meeting market orthodoxy head on), appears an eminently reasonable working solution, but it still poses structural planning dilemmas for capitalism. These are usually only solved during periods of acute 'total' warfare. The present problem is that the enemy is still over the horizon and doesn't yet appear at the gates, or the right gates, to get the troops in line. Furthermore, the battalions have to be internationally raised and coordinated, and will have to forgo the usual rapine. And as if to cap it all, the generalissimo volunteering for command appears to be (according to the *Guardian* at least) Tony Blair – God help us! *Heat* does not address the question of political practicalities but let's hope George is right and that 'people's power will save the planet'.

John Daniels

Ocalan

Abdullah Ocalan translated by Klaus Happel, *Prison Writings: The Roots of Civilisation,* Pluto Press, 336 pages, hardback ISBN 978-0745326160, £25

Abdullah Ocalan was the leader of the PKK, the Kurdistan Workers' Party, which conducted a guerrilla war from 1984 with the aim of establishing an independent Kurdish state in south-east Turkey. In February 1999, he was kidnapped on the way to Nairobi airport and taken back to Turkey, where he was tried and sentenced to death, although the sentence was commuted to life imprisonment.

In prison on the Turkish island of Imrali in the Sea of Marmara, he has produced, as part of a submission to the European Court of Human Rights, a volume which is an analysis of the history of civilisation centred, in particular, on the Middle East. Although his approach is essentially Marxist, he rejects economic determinism as the basis for his interpretation of history and places great importance on ideology. This is reminiscent of the Italian Communist, Antonio Gramsci, who also produced important theoretical work while in prison.

Ocalan regards the palaeolithic period of history, which covered 98 per cent of humanity's existence on earth, as having been brought to an end by the neolithic revolution, based upon better tools, the development of agriculture and animal husbandry. The essential counterpart to these technological changes was the development of primitive patterns of social behaviour such as fetishism, animism, totemism, matrilineal kinship, patriarchy, and so on.

The next technological revolution led to an oriental slave society. This was based on the use of bronze and the building of settlements which eventually became cities, initially on the Euphrates and Tigris rivers, before 3000 BC; in ancient Sumer. A vital feature of this revolution was the development by priests of a new ideology comprising a new religion and a new mythology. This was required to transform the mental outlook of the new settlers from one based on kinship and tribal freedoms to a submissive mindset in which slavery and inferiority were accepted. Citizens of Sumer were persuaded to accept subordination to a 'divine order' which reflected and demanded obedience to gods who, in effect, decreed a slave society. The priests established an ideological hegemony over the new urban settlements by this means.

Any challenge to this took a religious form. It was the will of alternative gods, monotheism or the advent of a messiah or redeemer which provided an ideological cover for a revolt, or even an invasion, from outside to overthrow a ruling élite.

Slave society with specific local features also developed in Egypt and the Indus Valley in the Indian sub-continent, and religious rituals and beliefs came into existence to create an acceptance of their structures. Elsewhere, other less advanced peoples went through the neolithic revolution before developing their own slave societies which were different in form though they embodied the same fundamentals as those to be found in Sumer. Greco-Roman societies did not have as rigid a religious structure as Mesopotamia or Egypt and, here, philosophical ideologies emerged.

Christianity and Islam both challenged slave society and provided the ideological counterpart to changes in the mode of production which led to the emergence of feudalism. Feudal society was basically concerned with land and land holdings, but it was dominated by religion.

Capitalism in its turn emerged through the introduction of new technologies and the scientific method, but it was accompanied by a successful ideological challenge to feudal religious dogma. In Europe this took shape as the Renaissance, followed by the Reformation, which led on to humanism, the enlightenment, individualism and secularisation.

Ocalan's view is that the Middle East failed to undergo an equivalent change. He believes it is in desperate need of its own Renaissance or Reformation, leading to the adoption of individual rights, secularisation, women's rights, pluralism and democracy. Only then can it advance.

He is committed to a socialist transition of society worldwide, but argues that this cannot be achieved by means of revolutionary violence or the establishment of a totalitarian state. He regards the Soviet Union as a failure in its overall efficiency, its excessive bureaucracy, and its denial of its peoples' rights. He further declares that traditional violent methods of achieving change have done extreme harm to the Arabs, the peoples of Israel, Iran and Iraq, and the Kurds.

He now argues that socialism can only be achieved through a wide-ranging democratisation and the achievement of a form of democracy which is superior to current Western democracies. He demands pluralist structures, participation of all in decision-making, women's rights, and peace.

'In my opinion', he says, 'one of the fundamental criteria characterising a socialist regime must be the level of democracy which it enables'. [p. 37]

Ocalan's treatise is based upon a profound study of the history of the ancient Middle East and the world in general. During the First World War a Belgian historian, Henri Pirenne, wrote a *History of Europe* to 1550 without access to sources, while he was interned by the German authorities. Ocalan's achievement in prison conditions, with limited access to books, calls this to mind, although he does provide a bibliography and, presumably, consulted the items listed.

Ocalan might have made some reference to the controversy about the existence of a specifically Asiatic hydraulic form of society, which Marx and Engels accepted, but which was rejected in the former Soviet Union. He might have referred to the theory of the former Iranian Kurdish leader, Abdul Rahman Ghassemlou, that the Kurds are the descendants of the Medes. There are numerous other aspects of his book that raise key issues for further discussion and debate. Some of his contentions are controversial.

Notwithstanding this, Abdullah Ocalan has produced a brilliant theoretical study of the origins and development of civilisation which should be essential reading for all historians interested in a scientific approach to our knowledge of the past. It is a fascinating work which is likely to be of permanent interest. The final conclusion that democratisation, not Islamic fundamentalism or the armed struggle (apart from self-defence), is the way forward in the Middle East and elsewhere is not the message one would expect to receive from the leader of a group that conducted a guerrilla struggle in Turkey for nearly a generation. Left-wing socialists and all who oppose imperialist attempts to dominate the world should consider very carefully the arguments which he advances to justify this thesis.

As for the Kurds, he suggests that being divided between several nations (i.e. Turkey, Iran, Iraq and Syria) gives them a key advantage in contributing to change in the Middle East by democratising themselves.

'No longer will the fate of the Kurds be ignorance, war, rebellion and destruction but a democratic and developed civil society and unity in freedom,' he declares. [p. 297]

Abdullah Ocalan has written an extremely important book which everyone concerned with the politics of the Middle East, the Kurdish question, ancient history or socialist ideas should read and digest. Whatever the view taken of his previous stance as a guerrilla leader, his erudite and thought-provoking thesis is of outstanding interest and I recommend it without reservation.

Stan Newens

Slobodan Milosevic

John Laughland, *Travesty: The Trial of Slobodan Milosevic and the Corruption of International Justice,* Pluto Press, 232 pages, hardback ISBN 9780745326368 £50.00, paperback ISBN 9780745326351 £14.99

John Laughland's superb new book, *Travesty: The Trial of Slobodan Milosevic and the Corruption of International Justice,* is the fourth important critical study of the issues pertaining to the Balkans wars that I have reviewed. The earlier three were Diana Johnstone's *Fools' Crusade* (2002), Michael Mandel's *How America Gets Away With Murder* (2004), and Peter Brock's *Media Cleansing: Dirty Reporting* (2005). It is an interesting and distressing fact that none of the three earlier books has been reviewed in any major US paper or journal, nor, with the exception of *Z Magazine* (and *Swans* and *Monthly Review*, which later ran a fuller version of the Johnstone review), in any liberal or left journal in the United States (including *The Nation*, *In These Times*, *The Progressive*, or *Mother Jones*). This is testimony to the power of the established narrative on the recent history of the Balkans, according to which Clinton, Blair and Nato fought the good fight, though coming in late and reluctantly, to halt Serb ethnic cleansing and genocide managed by Milosevic, with the bad man properly brought before a legitimate court to be tried in the interest of justice.

This narrative was quickly institutionalized, with the help of an intense propaganda campaign carried out by the Croatian and Bosnian Muslim governments (assisted by US PR firms), the United States and other Nato governments, the Nato-organised and Nato-servicing International Criminal Tribunal for the Former Yugoslavia (ICTY, or Tribunal), and the Western media, which quickly became co-belligerents in this struggle. This informal collective focused on numerous stories and pictures of suffering victims, on one side only and devoid of context. In commenting on the parade of witness victims, Laughland notes that 'Indictments [by the ICTY] are drawn up with little or no reference to the fact that the acts in question were committed in battle: one often has the surreal sensation one would have reading a description of one man beating another man unconscious which omitted to mention that the violence was being inflicted in the course of a boxing match.' But this stream of witnesses, that the defence could duplicate in its turn if given the opportunity – and Milosevic did with a video presentation of badly abused Serbs for several hours towards the beginning of his trial – is effective in demonisation and helped mass-produce true believers who viewed any contesting argument or evidence as 'apologetics for Milosevic'.

> 'Much ICTY funding comes from the United States government or its agencies such as the Orwellian sounding United States Institute for Peace. There has also been funding from George Soros' Open Society Institute ... Carla del Ponte rattled the begging bowl and said that the work of the ICTY was intended to deliver profits for private companies: "It is dangerous for companies to invest in a state where there is no stability, where the risk of war is high, and where the rule of law doesn't exist. This is where the long-term profit of the United Nations' work resides. We are trying to help create stable conditions so that safe investments can take place. In short, our business is to help you make good business ... international justice is cheap ... our annual budget is well under ten per cent of Goldman Sachs' profit during the last quarter. See, I can offer you high dividends for a low investment".'
>
> Page 28, *Travesty: The Trial of Slobodan Milosevic and the Corruption of International Justice* by John Laughland

This consolidation of a party line has been reinforced by a virtual lobby of institutions and dedicated individuals ready to pounce on both the deviants who challenge the new orthodoxy as well as the media institutions that on rare occasion allow a questioning of the 'truth'. The refusal to review these dissenting books and to deal with the issues they raise is also testimony to the cowardice and self-imposed ignorance of the media, and especially the liberal-left media, unwilling to challenge a narrative that is false at every level, as is spelled out convincingly in the three books reviewed earlier and once again in *Travesty*.

Laughland's *Travesty* focuses on 'The Corruption of International Justice' displayed in the Tribunal's performance in the seizure and trial of Milosevic, but in the process the book covers most of the issues central to evaluating the Balkan wars and the role of the various participants. The institutionalised lies are dismantled one after the next. On the matter of 'international justice', Laughland stresses the fact that the Tribunal is a political court with explicit political objectives that run counter to the requirements of any lawful justice.

This political court was organised mainly by the United States and Britain, countries that now freely attack others, but seek the fiction that will give their aggressions a *de jure* as well as quasi-moral cover. For this reason the rules of the Tribunal stood Nuremberg on its head. The Nuremberg Tribunal tried the Nazi leaders for their planning and carrying out the 'supreme international crime' of aggression. But the Tribunal Statute doesn't even mention crimes against peace (although with Kafkaesque hypocrisy it claims to be aiming at protecting the peace). Thus, Laughland notes, 'instead of applying existing international law, the ICTY has effectively overturned it'. The dominant powers now wanting to be able to intervene anywhere, the new principles to be applied were a throwback to the Nazis in disrespect for international borders. Laughland says that 'the commitment to non-interference in the internal affairs of states, reaffirmed as part of the Nuremberg Principles in the United Nations Charter, is an attempt to institutionalise an anti-fascist theory of international relations. It is this theory which the allies destroyed in attacking Yugoslavia in 1999'. And it is this anti-fascist theory that the Tribunal and humanitarian interventionists have abandoned, opening the door to a more aggressive imperialism.

The International Criminal Tribunal for the former Yugoslavia was established not by passage of any law or signing of an international agreement (as in the case of the International Court of Justice) but by the decision of a few governments dominating the Security Council, and Laughland shows that this was beyond the authority of the Security Council (also shown in another outstanding but politically incorrect and neglected work, Hans Kochler's *Global Justice or Global Revenge?* [Springer-Verlag Wien, 2003]). It was also established with the open objective of using it to pursue one party in a conflict, presumed guilty in advance of any trial. The political objectives were allegedly to bring peace by punishing villains and thus serving as a deterrent, but also to serve the victims by what Laughland calls 'the therapeutic power of obtaining convictions'. But how can you deter without a bias against acquittal? Laughland also notes that 'The heavy emphasis on the rights of victims implies that "justice" is equivalent to a guilty verdict, and it comes perilously close to justifying precisely the vengeance which supporters of criminal law say they reject'. 'Meanwhile, the notion that such trials have a politically educational function is itself reminiscent of the "agitation trials" conducted for the edification of the proletariat in early Soviet Russia.'

Laughland features the many-levelled lawlessness of the Tribunal. It was not created by law and there is no higher body that reviews its decisions and to whom appeals can be made. The judges, often political appointees and without judicial experience, judge themselves. Laughland points out that the judges have changed their rules scores of times, but none of these changes have ever been challenged by any higher authority. And their rules are made 'flexible', to give efficient results; the judges proudly noting that the Tribunal 'disregards legal formalities' and that it does not need 'to shackle itself to restrictive rules which have developed out of the ancient trial-by-jury system'. The rule changes have steadily reduced defendants' rights, but from the beginning those rights were shrivelled: Laughland quotes a US lawyer who helped draft the rules of evidence of the Tribunal, who acknowledges that they were 'to minimise the possibility of a charge being dismissed for lack of evidence'.

Laughland notes that the Tribunal is a 'prosecutorial organisation' whose 'whole philosophy and structure is accusatory'. This is why its judges gradually accepted a stream of rulings damaging to the defence and to the possibility of a fair trial – including the acceptance of hearsay evidence, secret witnesses, and closed sessions (the latter two categories applicable in the case of 40 per cent of the witnesses in the Milosevic trial). Tribunal rules even allow an appeal and retrial of an acquitted defendant – 'in other words, the Tribunal can imprison a person whom it has just found innocent'.

Laughland's devastating analysis of the Milosevic indictment and trial is a study in abuse of power in a politically-motivated show trial, incompetence, and faux-judiciary malpractice. The first indictment, issued in the midst of the Nato bombing war, on 27 May 1999, was put up in close coordination between the Tribunal and US and British officials, and its immediate political role was crystal clear – to eliminate the possibility of a negotiated settlement of the war and to deflect attention from Nato's turn to bombing civilian infrastructure (a legal war crime, adding to the 'supreme international crime', both here protected by this body supposedly connected to 'law' and protecting the peace!). The later kidnapping and transfer of Milosevic to The Hague was a violation of Yugoslav law and rulings of its courts. The Tribunal's Nato service and contempt for the rule of law was manifest.

The original indictment of Milosevic dealt only with his responsibility for alleged war crimes in Kosovo. But as Laughland points out, the wild claims of mass killing and genocide in Kosovo were not sustainable by evidence, and Nato bombing may have killed as many Kosovo civilians as the Yugoslav army. This accentuated the problem that if the Milosevic indictment was limited to Kosovo it would be hard to justify trying him for Kosovo crimes but not Nato leaders, a point even acknowledged by the Tribunal prosecutor. So two years after the first indictment, but after Milosevic's kidnapping and transfer to The Hague, the indictment was extended to cover Bosnia and Croatia. A bit awkward, given that back in 1995 when Mladic and Karadzic were indicted for crimes in Bosnia, Milosevic was exempted. There was also the problem that the Bosnian and Croatian Serbs were not under Serb and Milosevic authority after the declared independence of Bosnia and Croatia, and Milosevic fought with them continuously in an effort to get them to accept various peace plans 1992-1995 (documented in Sir David Owen's *Balkan Odyssey*, another important book neglected perhaps because of its contra-party line evidence).

So the prosecution sought to make the case for 'genocide' by belatedly making Milosevic the boss in a 'joint criminal enterprise' (JCE) to get rid of Croats and Muslims in a 'Greater Serbia'. The initial indictments that confined his alleged crimes to Kosovo never mentioned any participation in a 'joint criminal enterprise' or drive for a 'Greater Serbia'. So the prosecution had to start over in collecting evidence for the crimes, 'joint criminal enterprise', and Greater Serbia aims in Bosnia and Croatia and tying them to Milosevic. Guilt decision first, then go for the evidence, was the rule for this political court. The trial moved ahead while the 'evidence' was still being assembled. Most of it was the testimony of scores of alleged witnesses to alleged crimes, a large majority with hearsay evidence, and almost none of it bearing on Milosevic's decision-making or differentiating it from what could have been brought against Izetbegovic, Tudjman or Bill Clinton. Laughland shows very persuasively that the inordinate length of the trial was in no way related to Milosevic's performance – a lie beloved by Marlise Simons of the *New York Times* and the mainstream media in the Unite States in general – it was based on the fact that this was a political trial that inherently demanded massive evidence, and the prosecution, unprepared and struggling to make a concocted charge plausible, poured it on, trying to make up for lack of any documentation of their charges of a Milosevic-based plan and orders with sheer volume of irrelevant witnesses to civil warfare and Kosovo-war crimes and pain.

A key element in the prosecution case was the belated charge that Milosevic was involved in a 'joint criminal enterprise' with Serbs in Croatia and Bosnia to get rid of non-Serbs by violence, looking towards that Greater Serbia. The concept of a 'joint criminal enterprise' is not to be found in prior law or even in the Tribunal Statute. It was improvised to allow the finding of guilt anywhere and anytime. You are part of a 'joint criminal enterprise' if you are doing something bad along with somebody else, or are attacking the same parties with somebody who does something bad. With that common end you don't even have to know about what that somebody else is doing to be part of a 'joint criminal enterprise'. Laughland has a devastating analysis of this wonderfully expansive and opportunistic doctrine, and his chapter dealing with it is entitled 'Just convict everyone', based on a quote from a lawyer-supporter of the Tribunal who finds the 'joint criminal enterprise' a bit much. Milosevic probably would have been convicted based on this catch-all, or catch anyone, doctrine. Of course, it fits much better the joint and purposeful Clinton, Blair, Nato attack on Yugoslavia, or the Croats US-supported ethnic cleansing of Serbs from Croatian Krajina in August 1995, but there is nobody to enforce the 'joint criminal enterprise' against them, whereas we have the Tribunal to take care of US and Nato targets!

Laughland has a fine chapter on Greater Serbia, which shows that Milosevic didn't start the break-up wars (even quoting prosecutor Nice admitting this), that he was no extreme nationalist and that accusations about his speeches of 1987 and 1989 are false, that his support of the Serbs in Croatia and Bosnia was fitful and largely defensive, and that he was not working toward a Greater Serbia but at most trying to enable Serbs in a disintegrating Yugoslavia to stay together. During Milosevic's trial defence, Serb Nationalist Party leader Vojislav Seselj claimed that only *his* party sought a 'Greater Serbia', as the Croats and Bosnian Muslims were really Serbs with a different religion and his party fought to bring them all within Serbia – Milosevic only wanted the Serbs stranded in the breakaway states to be able to join Serbia. At that point the prosecutor Geoffrey Nice acknowledged that Milosevic was not aiming for a Greater Serbia, but, in Nice's words, only had the 'pragmatic' goal of 'ensuring that all the Serbs who had lived in the former Yugoslavia should be allowed ... to live in the same unit'. This caused some consternation among the trial judges, as Milosevic's aggressive drive for a Greater Serbia was at the heart of the Tribunal case. You never heard about this? Understandably, as the *New York Times* and mainstream media never reported it, just as they never tried to reconcile Milosevic's support of serial peace moves with his alleged role as the aggressor seeking that Greater Serbia.

There is much more of value in *Travesty* and I can't do it justice even on the issues discussed here. This is a wonderful book that should be on the reading list of everyone looking for enlightenment on the confused and confusing issues involving the Balkan wars and 'humanitarian intervention'. It helps shred the notion that the Nato attacks were based on a morality that justified over-riding sovereignty and international law, and it shows decisively that the Tribunal is a completely politicised rogue court that is a 'corruption of international justice'.

As Laughland emphasises (and Johnstone and Mandel do as well), the Nato war and the work of the Tribunal in running interference for that war, were very helpful in setting the stage for George Bush's wars in Afghanistan and Iraq and possibly, also, Iran. It was treated then, and remains treated today, as a 'good war', a 'humanitarian intervention'. So those who swallowed the standard narrative, built on lies, at best failed to see the continuity between Clinton and Bush, and the service of the former and the publicists of the 'good war' in removing the protection of the 'anti-fascist theory of international relations' that protected small countries from Great Power aggression, and unleashing the rule of the jungle.

Edward Herman

* * *

Michael Barratt Brown adds:

The trial of Solobodan Milosevic went on for four whole years, from February 2002 until his death in his cell in The Hague on 11 March 2006. It accumulated 50,000 pages of transcripts and the evidence of 300 witnesses with masses of files, DVDs, exhibits and documentation. Even a cursory reading of this material, which

I attempted while the trial was proceeding (see my Spokesman pamphlet *The Trial of Slobodan Milosevic*, 2005) revealed that the attempt to pin responsibility for genocide on Milosevic and the Serbian Government was failing. Much more authoritative judgment came later from the International Court of Justice to which the Government of Bosnia and Hercegovina had appealed.

The announcement by the World Court represents a very serious conviction of the Bosnian Serb army, but it leaves Milosevic and the Serbian Government unconvicted of complicity in or commissioning a genocide while criticising their failures to prevent genocide or punish it. What John Laughland's book then makes clear is what he calls 'the travesty of justice' in the very establishment of the International Criminal Tribunal for the former Yugoslavia and in its procedures and above all in the attempt to undermine the very basis of international law. In ten short chapters he exposes one by one the falsity of the claims made by Nato to justify the bombing of Yugoslavia.

The moral of this whole Yugoslav story is that such an attack of one state upon another, unless authorised by the United Nations, remains illegal and no appeal to 'higher law' can justify it. For any state, however powerful, to claim such higher authority undermines the whole basis of international law. This is what the United States has claimed, first in Yugoslavia, then in Afghanistan and Iraq – a new world order in which, as the first Chief Prosecutor of the Tribunal, Louise Arbour, put it, 'We have passed from an era of cooperation between states to an era in which states can be constrained'. We are left with the frightening question 'Where next?'